This book was originally published as *Why now. Omdat je prospects gisteren al klant hadden moeten zijn*, LannooCampus, 2022.

D/2022/45/380 – ISBN 978 94 014 88402 – NUR 808

Cover and interior design Chaomatic-Feline Godon and Adept vormgeving
Translation: Lynn Butler

LannooCampus Publishers is a subsidiary of Lannoo Publishers, the book and multimedia division of Lannoo Publishers nv.

LannooCampus Publishers
Vaartkom 41 box 01.02
3000 Leuven
Belgium

P.O. Box 23202
1100 DS Amsterdam
Netherlands

www.lannoocampus.com

MICHAEL HUMBLET

WHY NOW?

Because your prospects
should have been
customers yesterday

Lannoo
Campus

CONTENTS

Contents

Why this book? And why just now?   6

1   Problem
Under pressure: how to create your Why Now   12

2   Attention
For better conversion: follow the arrowed path   46

3   Trust
No more slick talk: showing your worth   84

4   Structure
Fit for a model: this is how you put your solution on the table   112

5   Next Actions
What's it gonna be: this is how you determine the next steps   138

6   The Ultimate Flow
Close (but no cigar): how to glue your Sales Story together   152

7   #Justaskmichael
Say Michael, and what about use cases?   170

Outro   188
Thank you   190
References   192
The Sales Story Rulebook   202
About the author   203

WHY THIS BOOK?

Why this book? And why just now?

Well, because of sales pitches like this:

Good morning. Hey, John and Britt, right? Good. Good. Great to come and pitch to you guys so early in the day. Hope you guys will stay awake. (Laughs)

So, I'm going to talk about my product X. A winner. You'll see. But it might be useful if first I tell you about myself. It's a bit easier to talk about myself anyway. So, I'm Steven and I've seen my share of meeting rooms. Like, a lot of them. I have twenty years of experience in various industries, so I know what makes a good product. So, I'm not going to sell you any nonsense. I promise you. Before I started my career, I did an internship with Jan from Very Large Company Y. Before that I interned at an Education programme, and even back then, everyone said I was a born salesman because I always got my way. (Winks)

But look, so, here I am now with you presenting my own product. This is my big dream. I've walked through the trenches to get to this point. Trust me. All this is possible because my product really works. Over the next one and a half hours you'll learn all about it. Naturally, I'm going to give you a brief explanation of how it works. After all, that's why we're here. But because one picture says a thousand words, I'll show you pictures of each of our offices, so you can also see my working environment. Especially our new office in Dubai. It really is worth a closer look. We've made a video about it that I will show to you later in my pitch.

By the way, I don't make product X on my own, I'm not that good. (Another wink.) So I mustn't forget the team of engineers and IT guys who back me up. Except for Femke. She also stands behind me, but as one woman.

So, before we start let's be clear about what you can expect from this meeting. First, I'll do a short introduction, then a word about my background and where my passion comes from and then the crazy story of my product and how we developed it. I'll give you all the details straight away because it is the details that make my product so special.

Next, my team will introduce themselves and then, of course, there will be a demonstration of how my product works. I have deliberately kept the presentation brief so that you will have a chance to ask questions during the final ten minutes. But no need for panic. I'll send you a copy of my slides and I have product brochures for you. Otherwise, are there any questions now? No? Then we can start with a short video on our Brussels office. Roll it!

This doesn't work

Your prospects have changed. Have your sales techniques changed too?

A sales pitch like the one above just does not work anymore. I wonder if it ever did? A sales pitch does not begin with a logo slide and end automatically with a closed deal an hour later. What your customer wants to hear is a story. A 'Sales Story'. A story that focuses on their needs and shows them how their business would benefit from your product or service.

Maybe your prospect does not need your solution today. That is not a problem because you are patient. You know your prospect might call you the moment they do need you. You will be there, with solutions designed for them.

You are probably thinking, 'I have a good product. There is interest in my product. I have made offers, hundreds of them.' And yet after your sales pitches, you are often met with ... silence. No response. Or much less of a response than you would like. This leaves me with one question: WHY would a customer buy your product or service NOW? If you do not have an answer, or if you can only come up with an answer after mulling over the question, then your Sales Story does not have traction. This problem is widespread and was present in 90% of my clients' companies before I began to work with them.

I have helped companies transform over five hundred sales pitches into highly effective Sales Stories over the last five years, in addition to teaching this subject at conferences and on numerous webinars. The basis of my approach to building a Sales Story is my *Why Now Model*, where a focus on five elements is needed to convert prospects into customers:

- **Attention**
- **Problem**
- **Trust**
- **Structure**
- **Next Actions**

Consideration of these five elements eventually coalesces into a single concept, a flow of information, tailored to each client.

If you have ever seen me in a webinar or on a stage demonstrating the use of my *Why Now Model*, you will know that I am a pragmatic person. In my view, the proof of the pudding is in the eating. That means that this book is not full of pure theoretical strategies. It describes real-life cases where my time-tested *Why Now Model* has yielded effective solutions for my clients. Before and after case studies are used to illustrate the weaknesses of conventional sales pitches and how to overcome them.

This book is not intended as a substitute for a lecture or a training course. I have already given plenty of those. Instead, it provides a blueprint for making your sales pitch, presentation, website, and brochure ... sharp. It is intended for everyone, in any setting, to develop and fine-tune their Sales Story and, overall, to convert sceptical prospects into loyal customers.

It took me a long time to finally write this book. The many questions I get every day about my *Why Now Model* finally made me stop procrastinating. Why now? Because your prospects expect something much better than the pitch described above. This book captures all my experience and knowledge, both theoretical and practical so that you can develop your own ultimate sales process. Get your pitches right from the very first contact. Get your Sales Story on point from the very first letter.

It is closing time.

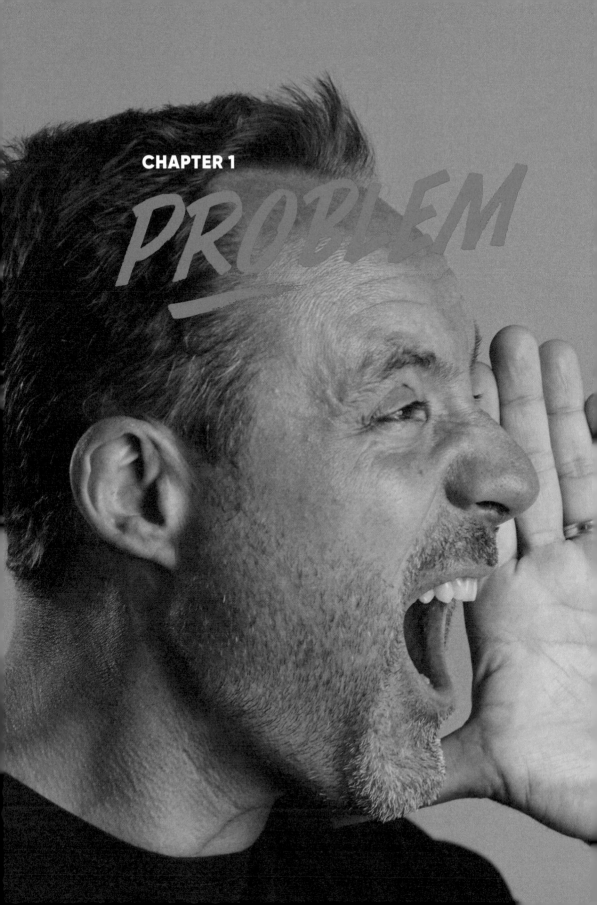

CHAPTER 1

PROBLEM

Under pressure: how to create your Why Now

'**M**ichael,' you may be thinking, 'there are no problems. There are only challenges.' That is fine for a book about coaching, but what you are holding in your hands is a book about sales. You need to get your prospects to the Next Action, in other words, one step closer to a sale. You are building a relationship here, you know.

Now then. Problems. Problems can be used to your advantage. A good sales pitch defines your prospect's problems in a way that builds intrinsic pressure for your prospect to find a solution. Why should your prospect buy your product at this time? How do you make them feel that internal pressure requires them to jump on the bandwagon ASAP, no hanging about, snap to it? That is what the *Why Now Model* is all about.

If I tell you what to do, you probably will not do it. That is human nature, and prospects are no exception. You can say 'buy now' but that will not make a prospect do it. They will want to do things their way which usually means they will do nothing.

That 'nothing' is the major stumbling block in social selling (bringing in leads by addressing prospects directly via social media). Despite the attractive scalability of digital social selling, the impassiveness of your target audience has equal scalability. No-response is now the norm with social selling, but it is just as problematic with other types of selling.

What can you do to avoid the Big Nothing? Well, you can create pressure or push them. Not a good idea. The pressure that people put on themselves elicits intrinsic motivation. You are more likely to train for a marathon because *you* want to do it than because your sweetheart thinks you need to exercise. You want your prospects to be motivated by intrinsic pressure. Nurture this by helping your prospects to understand that they need your solution and that they need to act now. You will not be successful if you take a commanding stance towards your prospects, call them frequently or tell them what to do. Be subtle but be clear and make some irresistible suggestions

A strong internal motivator is the famous FOMO (Fear of Missing Out), but there are other techniques. Use a variety of techniques to encourage your prospects to move in the direction you want. A description of these techniques and an explanation of how to use them to build in and accelerate pressure (the Now part of the *Why Now Model*) appears later in this chapter.

The shortest sales lesson ever

Selling is very simple. After all, there are only three possibilities with sales. You will be either

1. Too early
2. Perfectly on time
3. Too late

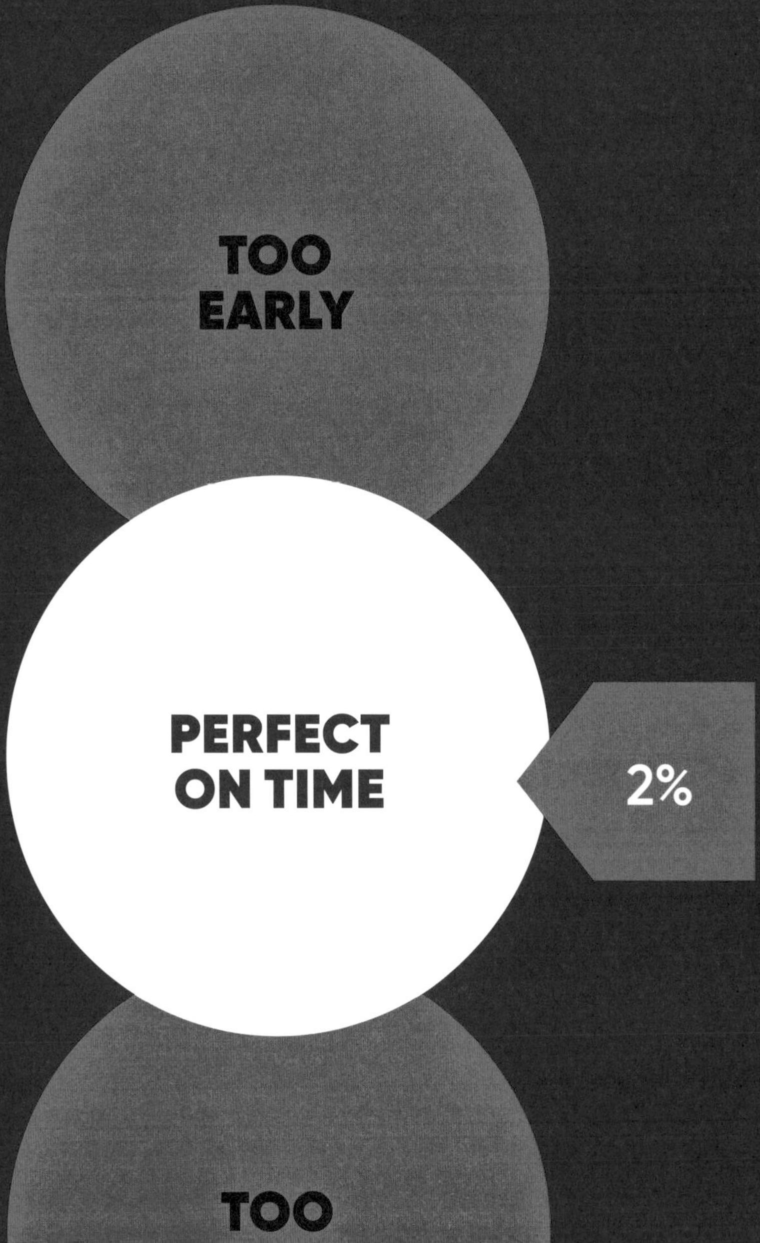

TOO
EARLY

PERFECT
ON TIME

2%

TOO
LATE

If sales is so simple, then why is the internet teeming with sales gurus claiming that they have found the ultimate sales method? Why have film clips of sales pitches reached icon status, like the 'Sell me this pen' skit from *Wolf of Wallstreet* or Alec Baldwin with his 'ABC' sales method (Always Be Closing) in *Glengarry Glen Ross*? Because they are pretty good methods, but only IF YOU **arrive at exactly the right moment**: that brief sliver of 'the moment' when your prospect already needs a solution like yours and you are lucky enough to be there to sell it.

Like George.

Panic! George's house is on fire. The good news: you sell fire extinguishers.

George feels extreme intrinsic pressure to solve his problem. He knows what his problem is and what the consequences could be. The *Why Now* of your fire extinguisher is irrefutable. When you stand at George's burning door with a competitor, you should debate value (keep it short though, think of poor George). Who has the best value proposition? Is the green or red extinguisher better? The one with powder, water, air or foam? It is certain that George will buy one or the other.

But what if you are too early? What if there is nothing wrong with George's house when you arrive? Would you be able to sell him a fire extinguisher at that moment? Possibly if you are good at 'cold' prospecting: cold calling, cold mailing, cold visits, cold outreach on socials ... But you will need to be a magician: cold sales have a conversion rate of less than 2.4% (on average, across all industries).

In most cases, salespeople present their sales pitch too early, missing out on a huge potential. (Too late is also possible, but other books have been written about that). It is essential that you use other techniques for prospects who are not urgently looking for what you are selling. Your Next Actions – a next appointment, please – are radically different than for George and his house on fire.

Beware: if you are too strident about closing the deal, you should be prepared for an (ice cold) 'no'. The Inuits may have 35 words for snow, but we people are very creative when saying 'no' in 35 different ways: just make me an offer; I'll call you later; yes, interesting; feel free to forward the slides; I'll put it to my colleagues or icy silence. Rejection is commonplace in sales. But there are ways to avoid losing your self-esteem and your prospect.

Sales is like swimming in a lake of rejection

With only a sliver of a chance that you will land in front of your prospect at just the right moment, you must bet on one of the two remaining choices for the timing of your pitch: too early or too late. Skip this step and you increase your chance of drowning in a lake of rejection.

Arriving with your pitch too late has obvious disadvantages, so with only one choice left, I will focus on arriving early with your pitch. The most efficient route to sales is to make an early connection with your prospect and carefully grow the relationship over time (nobody likes pushy). The success of this approach is demonstrated in B2B, where most deals are closed by roughly the fifth meeting. So, relax, you do not have to push for closing at the end of meeting one. Instead, you want to get your prospects to your Next Action (the next meeting). A relaxed next meeting with ample time and sandwiches. And with the case studies in this chapter.

Phew! Time for the basics in the shortest sales lesson ever.

There are 27 or so well-known trends in sales methodologies. New ones appear every day. If you have plans for world conquest through B2B sales, three of these are particularly relevant for the *Why Now Model*.

'Sales is like
swimming in the
lake of rejection'.

SALES METHODOLOGIES

1.

Solution Selling

Customers already understand their problem and want sales to address specific issues with products and services. Customers buy in days to **weeks**.

2.

Consultative Selling

The customer does not fully understand the problem. Sales has to diagnose the customer's situation to determine the right solution. Sales can take **6-18 months**.

3.

Provocative Selling

Sales experts can identify clients who will face a problem before the client themselves knows. They provoke an executive client into action. Often applied to innovative solutions, this B2B sales methodology takes anywhere between **3 to 9 months**.

Solution selling (solution-oriented selling)

In the 20s (that is nineteen-hundred and twenty, so more than one hundred years ago), Dale Carnegie wrote the book: *How to Make Friends and Influence People*. It is so modern in outlook that it could easily be an Instagram manual. He describes techniques that we now call 'solution selling'.

Let us examine the case where the prospect comes to you with a problem. **They have done their homework, diagnosed the problem and they understand in detail what solution** is required. This suggests that they have examined the solutions offered by your competitors and may have already met with them. All you need to do is position your value more strongly than the competition. Because value is the only thing that you really own.

The advantage of solution selling is that it moves projects quickly forward with a sales cycle of a few days to weeks. The disadvantage is that your prospect already knows a lot and can compare solutions. This makes it difficult to stand out in a competitive market. If you fail to do so, your margins will come under pressure (margin erosion, for those who want the right term) and the consequences can be disastrous.

Most sales training courses focus on this technique, with 'Sell me this pen' being a poster child example. Salespeople may go out on a limb and wave the puniest USPs around trying to prove the added value provided by their solution. They often make the mistake of overexplaining to the point that they exhaust their prospect and lose the sale. Nobody has time to listen to the glories of 28 features. Despite detailing your product's USPs, the sale may still go to your competitor with the highest award factor or the best-sounding name (hence the saying: 'No one has ever been fired for choosing IBM').

'But Michael, it won't always be that bad, will it?'

I know, solution selling sounds super straight-forward. But that is not the reason why this technique is used.

I once lost a big software deal to a well-known consultancy firm. We had quoted €250,000 for software that would fix their problem at that time and in the years to come. The board was not convinced. They asked for a thorough review of our quote and confirmation that we were the market leader. The cost of that homework? I guess it was about €1,000,000. They ended up purchasing a software solution from ... us. Without that huge diversion, I probably would not have won the contract, but still.

Sounds passé, selling this way? A bit, yes. Also, the technique has drawbacks: conversion and hit rates are low. But when all the elements are in your favour, it works very well and so this technique is still being used. I expect that solution selling will diminish as technology enters a more mature phase. In addition, the internet provides a gateway to information and the gate is wide open. Plus, the number of customers seeking less classical solutions is increasing. Innovation sells.

Consultative selling (Advisory selling)

A major change in selling came in the 1980s with the rise of big consultancy firms that developed consultative selling. It works as follows:

Your prospect knows something is wrong, but they cannot quite put their finger on what exactly the problem is. In many cases, they have the feeling that they should be able to do better or that they have missed opportunities to do better. Your prospect seeks help from experts and has come to you: the big consultancy firm. Consultative selling begins with an analysis to identify and characterise the problem, so selling that analysis and then performing it is the first step. Surprise, surprise: the consultants invariably find that, yes, there is a problem and praise be, the consultancy firm has a service or product that can solve the problem in no time. Magic!

The big advantage of consultative selling: services can be offered on a long-term basis, and you can embed yourself deeply into your client's organisation. From the moment you arrive, you have a huge competitive advantage to find and solve new problems for your clients. (You have come across embedded consultants. They are the ones sitting next to you at meetings who do not like any of your proposals).

The big disadvantage of consultative selling is enormously long sales cycles. Workshops, analyses, building credibility … It all takes its time. A POC (a proof-of-concept study or pilot study) is often needed to demonstrate feasibility, and this also takes time. Overall, it takes between nine and 18 months to close a consultative selling deal.

Provocative selling (provocative selling)

Provocative selling emerged along with the explosion of start-ups and scale-ups around the year 2010. This was due in part to incubators, but also because the Apples and Tesla's of this world showed that it is okay to overturn existing models for the sake of innovation.

Start-up founders or salespeople face a prospect in a very different way. They used to come up with a wildly disruptive story. Everyone wanted to hear that - nice, those young guys, cool ideas too - but no one wanted to buy the accompanying product or service. It smelled of risk.

Provocative selling is a technique that can allow you to push through a sale, even if the prospect thought he did not have a problem to be solved or had never even heard of the problem at all. You explain to your prospect that there is a UFO heading their way, an Unidentified Frightening Obstacle, and it is gaining velocity and becoming more frightening every moment.

The big advantage of provocative selling is that you come in with a sledge-hammer. Sledgehammers can be effective but not precise, so expect collateral damage. You need to pitch to decision-makers to be successful with this technique. If you pitch instead to a company's operations department, someone must report your story to the manager, the manager must take it to the CEO – like a Chinese whispering campaign that changes your story considerably as it is passed along. And what if someone in this communication chain thinks your solution plays to their disadvantage? You will have made an enemy which cannot be anything but counterproductive.

An efficient salesperson masters a mix of solution, consultative and provocative selling techniques. In the end, you never know exactly what stage your potential customer is in (too early, just in time, too late). You need to adapt your story to your timing. Choosing which sales technique to apply and when is the basis of the *Why Now Model*.

The *Why Now* Model

You now know the relationship between the situation your prospect is in and the selling technique that should work for them:

- Have characterised the problem and the type of solution they need – solution selling
- Have a hunch they have a problem, need it identified and solved – consultative selling
- Have no idea they have a problem, nor that they need a solution – provocative selling

These scenarios form the basis of the *Why Now Model*. Pretty simple, right? Optimise the use of the model by determining which stage your prospect is in relative to their problem. Let me illustrate this point with George:

How do you know what stage your George is in?

When a prospect comes to you asking for more info or a price, they at least acknowledge their problem. This means that, in theory, you will know at the outset what kind of soup is in the kettle. You will know to use solution selling or maybe consultative.

When contact is initiated from your side (cold, lukewarm or via referrals), you will not apply solution selling. Your potential customer does not yet recognise their problem, so you will move towards consultative or pro-vocative selling.

Practice, as is so often the case, is a little more nuanced.

These days, most high-velocity sales models focus on getting a foot in the door and then building a relationship and eventually trust. Hit and run is very 2000, we do not use that technique anymore.

High-velocity models, like our Why Now Model, work in steps: you seek connection at scale (digitally, that is), and you send valuable content that can help your prospect. This is how you start a conversation. During this conversation, you plant seeds for the future and ask questions to find out what stage your prospect is at. In this way, you find out how vigorously the house is burning, whether there is only smoke coming out or if nothing is happening yet. After these conversations, you know which Sales Story you will use.

The goal of the *Why Now Model* is to get your prospect to the Next Action. What that Next Action should depend on if they are ready to buy, or not ready to buy.

IF I WANT TO SELL TO YOU...

...what should I be talking about?

1. **Underestimated Problem**
The problem is far greater in magnitude and needs an alternative approach. They have underestimated the problem

2. **Unrecognised Driver**
The problem is driven by a different root cause than they realise. This way the problem is more manageable than previously thought

3. **Unforeseen**
An Unrecognised problem is fast approaching and it is worse than it seems and unlikely to disappear

Present a new way forward that only YOU can offer

Throughout your Sales Story, you will need to repeatedly remind prospects of cause-and-effect relationships. Encourage them to discuss their problem with you and help them to realise the effects it will have – and how your solution can help them. Learn to formulate their problem in a way that they recognise. You should then tailor your solution to fit their needs and describe it to them in terms that are meaningful to them. By using this approach, you will reduce friction, overcome resistance and stimulate the magic of intrinsic motivation. The key lies in refining how you formulate their problem and how that influences your solution.

With new clients it takes me two to three weeks and several iterations to find this key.

Since theory is only "in theory", I clarify each technique with a specific example from my own experience. Because what works, works.

Scenario 1: Your prospect understands their problem and knows the solution

In our theoretical example involving George, he comes to you and says: 'My house is on fire. I want a fire extinguisher.' You assess that your prospect already understands the problem and knows (often very well) what he needs. You can sense it: a case for the solution-selling technique.

Another example: your prospect is confident. Then you need to create misbalance and uncertainty. 'Is it only your house that is on fire? What if it spreads to the neighbours? What if you also have water damage afterwards from the fireman's hose?' By throwing your prospect off balance, you are breaching their sense of security, you sow doubt. You create an opportunity to offer an alternative approach to solve their problem: you share your expertise and provide guidance in the form of a solid approach, tried and tested, preferably cast in a neat model (more about those models at the end).

CASE STUDY

Solution selling – how to do it

Let me keep it very close to home. With my firm Chaomatic, we essentially solve three major problems:

1 Companies do not have time to create content. We shortcut their time by batch-producing content for them.
2 Companies have deep expertise, but no one knows it. We create content around all their knowledge and thus portray them as experts.
3 Companies do not know how to scale their expertise. We scale the distribution of their expertise.

Nine times out of 10, the client asks: 'Can you create a video about us?' In their head is a drone image of the company, which turns into an image of the CEO in his best suit telling the story of how good they are. The usual.

In fact, I get this question so often that we now feature it as the standard question on our website:

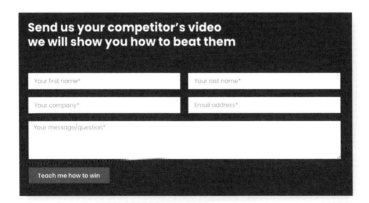

The company knows exactly what they want. They know what the problem is. It is just that they do not have the best concept in mind of how to portray it. This is where I begin with pure solution selling.

I ask questions about what direction they want that video to take. They usually then show me an example. I ask then how urgent the video is to learn the *Why Now* of the company. Then I repeat what they asked for:

'So, you want a video to get better known, generate more leads, create brand awareness?'

I probe around until I hit a sensitive spot, until I unearth a problem. I repeat their stated problem, clearly and matter-of-factly:

'But you also say you haven't made a video before because videos are expensive, and you don't know how to distribute the material to your target audience?'

If I immediately offer them a solution, I will demonstrate my value, but I will not position myself against the competition. They can very easily write to five other agencies and ask for prices. So, what do I do? I place their problem in a new light.

'Let's walk through it.' I reformulate their problems to fit perfectly with our three big solutions.

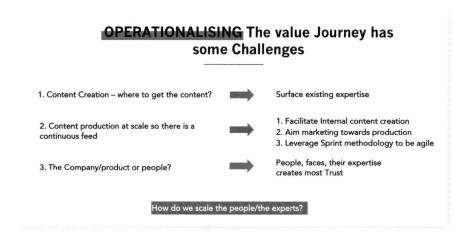

This is how I optimise and strengthen Chaomatic against the competition. I position us as unique by explaining that, with us, the potential client will not need a movie. Instead, we will provide them with a content machine, giving them enough content in one day to last them for months. And for the same budget as one video. What do they choose? Six months of content, or one video?

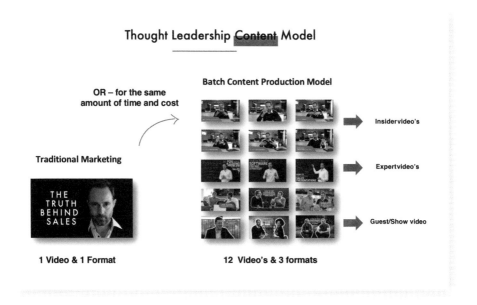

Scenario 2: Something is wrong – your prospect does not know what it is nor what to do

George is back: 'There is something wrong with my house. We smell smoke, but we don't know why or where it comes from. What do you think the problem is and do you have something to fix it?' Your prospect senses that there is a problem, but often they do not know exactly what is wrong and (it follows) have no idea of a solution. This scenario is best addressed by **consultative selling**.

If you try solution selling here, you will magnify the problem. As a result, your prospect will become doubtful, insecure and (sometimes literally) walk away, putting the brakes on your sales cycle. Therefore, it is very important to master different selling methods and to apply the right one where appropriate. In this case, you need to offer your prospect peace of mind and certainty: unburdening, as it is called.

You do this by showing that the problem has a different cause than what the customer thought. But also – sigh of relief! - that it is much easier and quicker to solve than first thought. You bring an uncertain client peace of mind, guidance and a concrete plan, focused on the future.

Consultative selling
– this is how you do it

Welcome to the world of learning software. Learning software offers platforms that allow clients to transfer, adjust and keep knowledge in their organisation on point. I ended up in the world of learning software at the request of an investor. I knew of its existence, but whether it was a big market? I had no idea. I learned that the European market consists of about 8,000 learning managers who are responsible for gathering, building and maintaining knowledge.

The investor wanted me to help one of his investees, a company that developed learning software, to improve the quality of their pitch materials and the skills of their sales team. This meant I would be meeting with people tohelp them to build their sales pitch, sales process and sales team.

Let me take you back to my first visit with a salesperson from the investee and one of their prospects. The salesperson, a learning expert with loads of experience, flew straight into it: 'Ms. Dewitte, as you know, there are three major categories of learning methods.' Prospect nods in agreement. 'Through our research, we have discovered a fourth, much more efficient method.'

This was followed by an intellectual debate unlike any other. I watched open-mouthed as the two experts pummelled each other with their knowledge. After an hour of discussion – briefly interrupted by a software demo – we stepped outside. I just observed the whole thing and asked afterwards if it went well. Affirmative: 'We are definitely going to get a sale.' I replied, 'There was certainly lots of enthusiasm. But what struck me was the client's non-verbal behaviour. That spoke volumes.' Ms Dewitte's posture said: 'Who do you think you are, explaining to me how to do my job?' The result? There was no deal, no project, no opportunity.

The model

Shocking would not have worked when pitching to Ms Dewitte. She was aware that things could have been done differently and done better. But she did not know what to do. If she had known what to do her company's problem would have been solved long ago. We needed to demonstrate to her that we could help her company find a path to the future: something that she felt safe with, yet added a bit of pressure (*Why Now*, right?) to encourage her to act quickly.

I held many meetings with my client's salespeople to try and understand the steps in their Sales Stories. I just could not make sense of their sales tactics. They kept droning on in detail about the 'pillars of learning' but I had no sense of the overall message of their pitches. Finally, I had no choice but to go for a pint with the company founder. I kept putting the same question to him: 'Where is this going? What are the steps and associated problems?' Twelve full beer mats later, I arrived at an answer.

Using my beer mats, I was able to map out a basic model he could use for his company's pitches. I planned a meeting for the CEO and myself with a completely new prospect. The CEO handled the intro, and I took over for the pitch. (Models are great, by the way, for such situations - more on this in Chapter 4.)

The meeting

'Let's talk about the different learning methods. Which is currently the best method? Most firms start with traditional learning. Like what we do now: I explain, and you listen. Knowledge has been imparted this way for centuries. But how accurately and completely is knowledge absorbed with this method? Hmm ... So, it is not an entirely reliable method. In fact, it is unreliable. How do we solve this?'

The prospect responded, 'Learning experts know the answer immediately: an e-learning platform.'

'Indeed. The advantages: digital e-learning platforms are scalable across regional branches and internationally, no one must be physically present, and we professionalise scale distribution. But the quality of e-learning is not predictable. We cannot confirm whether the learning has been effective. We do not know if it stuck. I say: but what if we add intelligence to this process? By adding more intelligence to a software we can make this learning predictable. We know what, when and where learning takes place. If we then have it analysed, we can understand how a large group learns. This way we can validate the knowledge. We are now working on the final step: together with a university, we are developing the algorithms of the future. We are evolving towards expert mapping to build full expertise.'

The right Learning Method

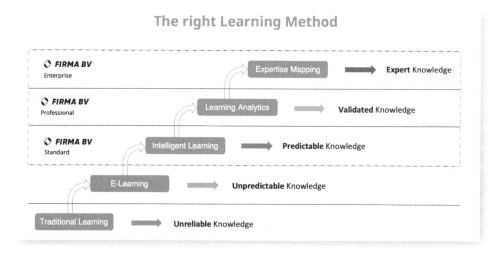

Our prospects were mostly in the first or second phase, meaning we met them 'right on time' or 'early' in their search for a solution. We showed them a clear causality by recapping their problem and showing them the negative outcome if they had no solution (here is a problem). Then we gave our pitch a positive spin when we presented our solution. We literally showed a path (or staircase) to the solution. Small steps because it is important to have everyone on board and the end goal must not seem insurmountable. It is important to paint an achievable scenario for your prospect that they can grow into.

In a subsequent slide, we offered different product licences for each of the different methods. Although original they only had one license but in order to fit these we had to offer choices. (This is a classic sales technique called anchoring. Read more about anchoring in the FAQS at the back of the book.) This distinction between the sets of features prompted the prospects to immediately ask what features were available under the most complete licence. At this point, the CEO picked up the discussion and explained the licence, which we eventually offered also as a light version (standard).

From then on, all salespeople were trained to transmit variations of the same Sales Story when they pitched to prospects. I made sure this was possible verbally, on paper and with slides.

Consultative selling – this is how to do it

One of the companies I worked with offers a blockchain platform. Blockchain ensures that data sourced from different contributors is stored anonymously, 100% authentic and verifiable to ensure there is no 'fiddling' or 'creativity' with data. The company was asked to give a presentation at a major IoT fair in the Middle East. I-what? IoT, or the Internet of Things, is the set of devices that interact and exchange data with other devices or systems via the internet. Everyday objects (your radio, lights, floor heating) that are connected to the internet can communicate with you and with objects and even make decisions. It is all very futuristic and extremely hi-tech.

The company asked me to create a different story. Their existing Sales Story was mainly about how to use blockchain to sell data from large construction projects or use it for more efficient projects. The company was way ahead of its time which resulted in them coming to prospects a bit too early.

You should know that almost all presenters at such a show do pretty much the same thing: a classic IoT slide with images of a lot of connected sensors in cars, buildings and mobiles doing magical things. Preferably with lots of blue, because that is how it is done in the hi-tech world.

I played the game and used a clichéd IoT slide as an opener. And then I said, 'STOP. You have heard this story before, haven't you? You've seen this a hundred times. It can be done differently.' So, I deliberately brought contrast into my presentation by pointing out what my audience would expect.

Now that I had their attention, I had to deliver. So, I flipped the standard presentation on its head. IoT companies present themselves as offering tools for cost-cutting: tap into sensors and collect, analyse and optimise data. Not exactly sexy. I said, 'What if the tables were turned and instead of talking only about costs, we talked about profits? What if my company's tools could enable an alternative business model?'

The most expensive part of a building is not its construction but its ongoing maintenance over 20 to 30 years. If I want to examine the cause-and-effect relationship of a decision to build or not to build I can proceed as follows: I list the negatives associated with taking a decision to build as depicted in the figure below. This compares the relative costs of constructing a building versus the cost of maintaining it.

Traditional Building models are a cost center

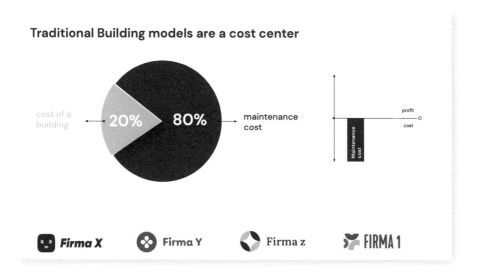

These slides were very different from what the other Keynote Speakers showed. Here both the problem and the solution were immediately tangible. The number of questions exploded after the presentation.

Moving from a cost to a profit center

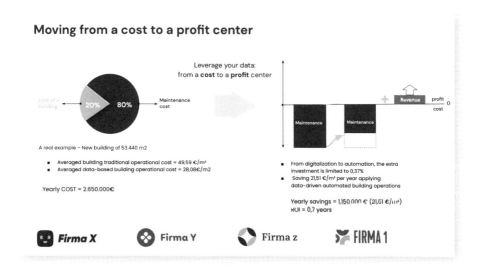

'Why is your presentation covered with logos?', you may ask. Well spotted. An audience will always make a link between logos and the rest of a slide. Even though the presenting company had none of those companies as clients at that time (they do now, no worries), the presence of recognisable logos added credibility. A subsequent research collaboration with a university has added further credibility.

Starting point 3: Your prospect does not have a problem

We visit George one last time. We tell him that his house might be on fire one day, so he had better take precautions. And although George doesn't know it yet, he does urgently need a fire extinguisher. This asks for **provocative selling**.

If your prospect believes that he does not have a problem, then despite our best efforts with solution selling, we will not make a sale. In such cases, we need to bring out our sledgehammer and our story will be: dear prospect you have a massive problem although you do not realise it, it is approaching faster than you dare suspect and it is not going to go away any time soon.

Provocative selling – this is how you do it

The real estate industry is characterised by long, complex processes and many administrative steps. A lot of steps means that a lot can also go wrong, that you need a lot of staff and that all those processes take up lots of valuable time.

The company in this case had built a software platform designed to ease the administrative burden of real estate brokers. Their objective was to eventually have every broker from a small or medium size firm working with their platform. Their CEO brought me on board to help with this.

On the first day, I asked their salesperson to make some cold calls. Listen in:

- Hi, I'm Jane from firm Y. Do your house sales involve a lot of administrative steps?
- Euh ... What do you mean? And who exactly are you?
- I'm Jane from firm Y. We built a software platform that can improve your workflow, simplify your process and reduce your overheads.

This is a classic shortcut approach: straight to the point, immediately talking about the product. You can probably guess how long these conversations lasted and what kind of success rate the salesperson had. It will come as no surprise to you that out of 20 phone calls, only one resulted in an appointment. I went along on that one appointment.

The saleswoman spent the entire appointment talking about herself and the product. In doing so, she used wild slides full of text, photos, Tesla pictures, images of high-end houses (which is a niche market), and logos and made comparisons to her competitor's technologies none of which the prospect was remotely familiar with. She explained the intelligence of her company's system, supporting this claim with busy drawings of flow diagrams to show the internal workings of the software.

After less than 10 minutes, the saleswoman completely lost focus but continued to ramble on for a full hour. The prospect kept glancing at his watch and trying desperately to wind up the meeting. How many deals came out of this combination of cold calls and meetings? Too few.

What were the saleswoman's biggest problems?

- Her sales story emphasised her deep technical knowledge
- She used terms that her prospects did not know
- She used sales techniques to pitch to other salespeople who caught on to her sales strategy – to be crystal clear

- Her value propositions were not sufficiently attractive to her prospects
- There was no urgency, no *Why Now* in her Sales Story
- Did I mention she talked mostly about herself and the product

So, Company Y was facing a sales problem. Fortunately, I had a solution.

First, evaluate the person you are pitching to. In this case, the client was an estate agent who was a smooth and very experienced seller. Estate agents are normally proficient in selling techniques and are - rightly - proud of their successes. In addition, they understand their complex administrative process very well. Besides closing deals, managing complex administrative processes is their core business. On the other hand, most brokers are not software specialists. They do not know that they can make their processes run more smoothly and what technology is available to achieve this.

I ruminated over the issue for a week, dug deep into the real estate market and came up with an idea. What if I used a provocative pitch? What if I talked to their prospects about their competitors, some that they were not even aware of, who were already using systems like my client's to take a leading position in the market? News of these competitors would hit them right in their wallets and tarnish their pride.

I called the next prospect on the list. Not to sell immediately - my Next Action was just to speak to the prospect in the office for ten minutes. Are you listening in?

- Hello, Michael here. Am I speaking to Bart?
- Yes indeed.
- Good to speak to you. Your agency is at location X, isn't it?
- Yes. What can I do for you?
- I am conducting a survey on successful real estate agencies. There is an agency in your area that grew 600% last year.
- ... (The cogs turn - who? What? Where? Lots of questions ...)
- Say, Bart. I will be in your area next Tuesday anyway. Shall I pop in for a short coffee to show you how they handled it?

The result? Eighteen out of 20 phone calls ended in an appointment. I had hit a sensitive spot.

The meeting

I took a presentation with me to the meeting. But I could have just as easily drawn the Sales Story on a sheet of paper or presented it verbally.

'Wonderful office,' I said as I walked in. We made our introductions and then I pounced.

'Most traditional real estate agencies (ouch, that stings, nobody wants to be traditional in this industry) have a heavy administrative process to deal with when they sell a house. You know the ones: ...'

I went through the steps with my prospect, which gave me a chance to ask a few questions, check things and raise issues. The broker saw that I under-stood him and his world.

4-5 hours per listing

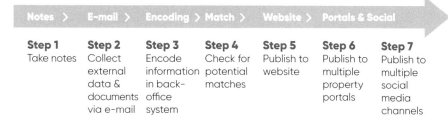

Notes >	E-mail >	Encoding >	Match >	Website >	Portals & Social	
Step 1	**Step 2**	**Step 3**	**Step 4**	**Step 5**	**Step 6**	**Step 7**
Take notes	Collect external data & documents via e-mail	Encode information in back-office system	Check for potential matches	Publish to website	Publish to multiple property portals	Publish to multiple social media channels

Then I moved on to the provocative bit: introducing information he did not yet have, something new and interesting. 'You are not alone in this process. Before we developed our software, we did a lot of research on its impact. Take a look at the figures: ...'

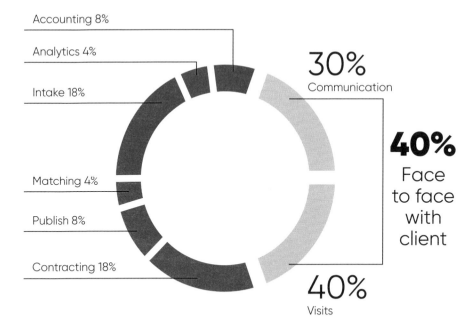

Accounting 8%

Analytics 4%

Intake 18%

Matching 4%

Publish 8%

Contracting 18%

30%
Communication

40%
Face
to face
with
client

40%
Visits

'As you can see, all the steps in your process have a negative impact on your time commitments. All those administrative steps leave you with very little time left for your customer. And where can you have most impact with your business? With the customer, that's where your real strength lies. In that connection, the human touch. That's where you make the difference, right?'

I then shifted up a gear. 'If we look at it in the abstract, you see that you spend a lot of time on slow administrative processes, which add little value. This means that only 40% of your total time remains to deal with your customer, despite that it is with your customer where you make a difference. All traditional offices have this problem.'

'Well, not all of them,' I continued. 'Remember the agency that grew 600%? This is their time allocation: up to 70% of their time is spent with clients. They have been able to reduce their low-value administrative tasks to the bare minimum.' That raised their eyebrows.

Traditional agency

Client time

40%
Face to face
with client

Low Value Tasks

'New' agency

Client time

70%
Face to face
with client

Low Value Tasks

Here comes the pitch.

'We at company Y are going to make sure you move from the left (limited time with the customer) to the right. More time with the customer, and less time spent on low-value tasks. The result: more sales faster and a bigger market share.'

Not once did I explain the technology or use words like 'workflow'. My Sales Story was only about them and their problem: the before and after. I was showing them a way forward for their business.

The result

After sixteen appointments, we signed twelve deals. That Sales Story worked.

These meetings included, of course, concrete explanations of how the solution worked, but I deliberately kept the technical descriptions brief with not too much detail. I had ten minutes, remember? The goal was the Next Action: a next meeting. Thanks to short meetings in which you do not push for a sale from the start, you create opportunities for more contact and develop trust. You can go into further detail about how the product works in a future meeting.

Disclaimer

This pitch worked for small to medium-sized offices. I hit them right in the heart with a problem and a solution. However, when we presented the software to larger offices, the Sales Story did not work. The problem facing large offices was not administration, but control of their franchises. So be very aware of the prospect sitting in front of you. Be aware of where they sit in the company's hierarchy and what the company's business model is. These three elements help determine the problem you need to build your pitch around.

The big problem is not your prospect's problem

Large sums of money flashed before my eyes when I bought my house. Twenty thousand euros was added to the total and then €10,000 was subtracted. I did not question it much. I went for a coffee after signing the contract and complained that my coffee cost €4.50. Big amounts of money are abstract, small amounts you feel. Make use of this when you describe the prospect's problem.

Consider the following example.

A start-up developed a device that mechanically sews up the abdominal wall after surgery. In their pitch, they stated that - unlike the needle and thread of the last 3,000 years - this was much more efficient, hygienic and safe. An abdominal wall is logically sewn only at the end of an operation and the surgeon, also only human, is as this happen at the end of a long surgery often tired by then. Automating this step reduces the risk of errors to almost zero.

In their Sales Story, the start-up elaborated on this: the risk of mortality using manually implanted sutures is 1.2 million people worldwide. That number, 1.2 million, is obviously a big deal, but it is too abstract to be meaningful. It made more sense to quote a figure that was relevant to the surgeon such as the mortality rate for the country or region. My client could explain that their solution could make the surgeons in the hospitals more efficient, able to operate faster and treat more patients. This would benefit the bottom line (always important) meaning the hospital would generate more revenue. Plus, the incidence of ugly scar claims and related claims would be reduced.

Investors want to confirm that a given product has sufficient potential to make an investment interesting. This might tempt presenters who are pitching to investors to focus on major markets. But whether your pitch is to potential clients or investors, start with relevant numbers that your audience can grasp. In other words, zoom in on a problem to make it tangible and recognisable. Big numbers sound impressive, but do not underestimate the power of the small ones.

Conclusion: from now on, problems do exist. You can forget the notion that problems are only challenges. Your challenge is to expose your prospect's problem in all its glory. Do this in a way that makes your prospect feel that it is time to solve their problem and that action may be needed.

Problems do not have to be solved ASAP. The reality is that haste and urgency are rarely helpful in landing a sale. Your *Why Now*, your problem (or future problem) should be built slowly but surely. In most cases, your prospect will not need you yet, so do not expect them to call you tomorrow for a quote. Nor the day after tomorrow. But if you simply put the problem on the table, you will have created a growing and somewhat uncomfortable feeling in them but left them too with the knowledge that you have a solution. They may think, 'Maybe we should not wait too long after all? Maybe we should find out if that could be something for us.'

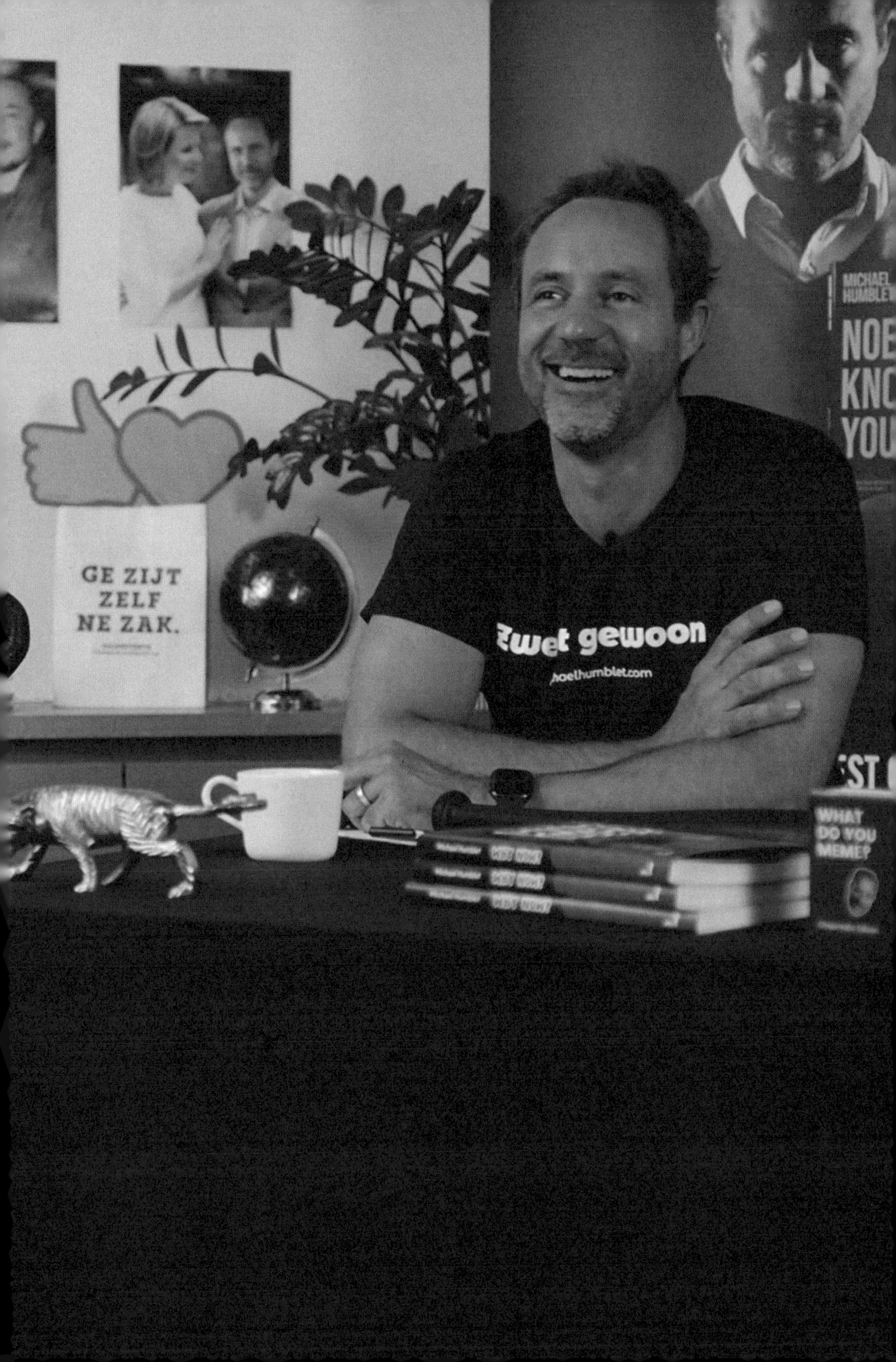
GE ZIJT
ZELF
NE ZAK.
WHAT
DO YOU
MEME?

CHAPTER 2

ATTENTION

For better conversion: follow the arrowed path

Hey Michael, check this out! Our sales presentation is amazing! Unique! Ground-breaking! There's a picture of our building, a cool logo, everything is explained in detail and there's even a quote from Elon Musk! We've nailed it. Right?

Hold it.

Two slides into a presentation like this I reach my limit, politely interrupt, and ask the presenter to stop. From start-ups to multinationals, and biotech to IT solutions, the problem of overly packed slides is rife. I have seen slides so filled with minute details about companies and quotes so cheesy they attract mice. Not to mention corporate videos. Ghastly.

Perhaps you have been enthusiastically pitching to prospects for over ten years. Yet you are not getting the results you hoped for. Weird, right? My question to you is:

What message do you want to get across with each slide in your deck? Is your audience supposed to remember something or just be impressed by the word count and visual violence?

Well. I am waiting. No answer? It seems you have never thought about this.

Another thing: what exactly should I be learning from your slides? All I see is a soup of letters and words, with a generic picture here and there, but no clear message. What do you want me to focus on? What conclusions should I draw? What is your take-home message?

Well, well. Again, no answer.

Apparently, you have so much to say that nothing is being said. You are not alone. Information overload in presentations is a common problem that almost every company struggles with. It is a common human response, but it is not efficient for sales.

I understand why this happens. I get it. After all, your company or your product is your baby. You are proud of it. Just like brand-new parents, you want to sing out the praises of your wonderful little one to the whole world. It is understandable that you want to blurt out every feature the moment you set your eyes on a prospect. You are convinced of its merits, so why should others not share your view? So, you drone on and on, ploughing relentlessly through every detail on every slide. Main points and side issues criss-cross as you zoom in on details to the degree that your audience loses all interest. Your genuine enthusiasm is so overbearing that you frighten your prospects, delay the deal or even make them jump ship. How regrettable.

'But Michael,' you are thinking, 'surely a bad pitch is mainly due to a bad product?'

Look, the following two firms sell top products, no doubt about it. But their pitches? Judge for yourself.

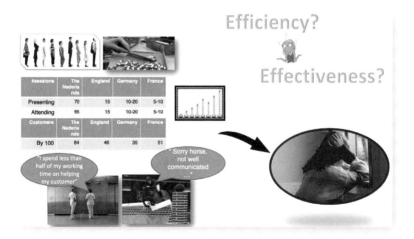

What you can expect from our Top Technology

- **Customer Centricity becomes a fact**
- **Increase reach and advocacy**
- **Continuous first hand data enrichment**
- **100% Traceability, GDPR and Compliance**
- **State of the art SAAS sales enablement technology**

Take a step back. Take another look at your service or product. This is the view that your prospects will have prior to your pitch. Focus on one vital question: what problem does your product solve? Return to basics: why does your product exist? Tell them less but tell them what matters.

- What problem does your prospect have?
- What will they conclude from your pitch?
- Where is the big red ball in your slide, the key message that cannot be overlooked?

Your customer has a problem, the conclusion should be that your product or service solves that problem. And the red ball? That is the attention-grabber on your slide. These three elements determine if your prospect will understand you: if they will remember the content, if they can and will retell your story internally.

Above all, avoid forcing your listener to work hard to understand your message. Their problem and your solution should be obvious and clearly depicted in your visuals. Complex slides packed with information are hard to process - the human brain is lazy by nature. If your pitch and your ideas are hard to understand, do you think your prospects will look forward to a collaboration with you?

I agree. The key is attention. Grab their attention at the right moment, hold on to it and focus it on what you want them to see. Fortunately, there are many science-based techniques for directing attention, and methods to lead your prospects to the 'Aha' experience you are hoping for.

First the theory: this is how attention works

Although societies and technologies are changing at a rapid pace, the functioning of our brains is still largely the same as that of our paleontological ancestors. If they saw something new, it got 100% attention: is this dangerous? Is it stronger than me? Can it eat me?

Now the chances are small that you will eat your prospects (I don't want to generalise), but our brains still work the same way. You are new. Your pitch is new. For the first few minutes, your audience is in a hyperfocus mode. Your prospects decide at that moment: is this interesting? Is it worth my attention? Can it benefit me?

These are your golden minutes, fill them only with essential info. You can delete that quote from Elon Musk on slide two. Why would you let him take your moment? Why give Elon the credits? You are the expert in this presentation.

Tips on how to ruin your presentations (and how to improve them from now on)

Attention is not something an audience gives you automatically, it must be earned. Except at the beginning as this is the one (or only) time when you will have their undivided attention. You are a novelty, and their minds are fresh and open. You must not squander that attention. You know this. So why do many speakers do one of the following in the first three minutes:

 ## Launch into a detailed autobiography, unrequested and of interest to no one

Yes, Steven, it is cool that you have worked with your company for four years, that you have two PhDs, bought your first Rolex at 16 and that you have been photographed with Mark Zuckerberg. That makes you seem stodgy to me. Your Rolex does not do much for me and Mark, frankly, he is history. What are you trying to prove? That you are credible? Okay. But then it might be more relevant to talk about your knowledge. And above all, I want a credible solution to my problem. Do you have one or not?

Traditional salespeople start with a summary of how many years they have been in the business, how many clients they have brought in, how many people they employ and where their offices are located ... not unlike Steven boasting about his expensive watch.

Does that mean you should not talk about yourself? If you read my first book, Nobody Knows You, then you know that this would never be my advice. But this is neither the time nor the place to sell yourself. Your personal credibility and legitimacy become relevant later in your story. For now, skip the bio. Present only crucial information in the first few minutes.

Introduce the team

The same category, but this time it is the team's biography, starting with the CEO who once had a brilliant idea and then worked his way up from nothing. Then there is Ciska from marketing, who is responsible for company culture, and we are cool because there is a ping-pong table in our office. Starting a presentation with these points is particularly common among start-ups. Sure, human capital is the most important asset at a start-up. But introducing the person who oversees company culture is, as the renowned cyclist Contador would say, of 'cero, cero, cero, cero, cero' importance to your prospects. Especially at the very beginning of your presentation.

An exception: if Jeff Bezos is on your team, you might mention that. But keep it for later.

Show or - even worse - read an agenda out loud

The presenter announces, 'In this episode of Temptation Island: Excitement! Temptation!' But the audience is neither excited nor tempted. Following a break in the pitch, the presenter repeats the promise. Again, there is no excitement and no temptation. Agendas create expectations. When it comes to presentations, the expectation is usually negative, 'Argh, this is going to take forever.'

Your sales meeting may surprise, and should continue to fascinate!

Agendas are a necessity for workshops and training courses. But for sales pitches, your goal is to get your prospect to the point of agreeing on a 'Next Action'. Not to the point of making a sale, but to an important step in the process of getting to know and trust one another. So, do not prime an audience, only to ultimately disappoint them. Your pitch should captivate the audience and keep them captivated. So do not waste precious time on a silly agenda. Skip it.

A deluge of details

Fussy features, unique design elements no one else has, the few milliseconds it takes your app to start up ... you fear not having enough to say so you do a data dump. You drown your audience in detail. It is a shame, but as you do this you watch their attention melt away like ice cream in the sun. This a classic example of information overload. You can see it on their faces. There is a reason why this phenomenon has its own acronym: WIIFM. What's in it for me?

Arrogance

Consultants and companies that offer smart technology make the mistake of playing their joker card at the outset of their presentations. I once worked as head of sales at a big data firm (am I making myself seem foolish here?). Our CEO had the following opening line for all his pitches 'Hello, I am X, founder and CEO of company Y and we employ eighty people with PhDs in mathematics. With this top-notch team ... blah-de-blah.' Impressive, sure, but it immediately set unrealistically high expectations. And what did the listener remember? That the CEO thought that he and his eighty people were much smarter than all those idiots sitting in front of him. The indignation on the faces of those 'idiots' was plain to see. Selling starts with mutual respect. In this case, it starts with you: respect is something you earn, it is not automatic.

Is it wrong to be proud? But yes. You can demonstrate later how incredibly well your solution solves your prospect's problem. You can also mention that a smart team is behind your solution. Street credibility and experience are often worth more than a wall full of diplomas.

You can now understand how easily and quickly you can lose the attention of your audience. Fortunately, you can also grab them with both hands from the very first minute. Whether you speak, draw, present slides or write to prospects, the following two techniques will seriously boost an audience's attention.

 # Talk about them

What is the objective of your sales pitch? You want your prospects to see the light and then act. You want them to get to know your product. It is all about them, not you. Focus on your target and talk about their problem and their needs. Use direct language to touch the depths of their corporate souls. You want them to feel that you understand them. Not by saying so, but by sharing your intimate knowledge about their industry and its pitfalls. You want to connect with them and gain their trust. How can you cultivate that intimate connection? I will explain this to you in Chapter 3 which addresses trust.

 # Start with the problem

Harmonious chords resonate. Talk about the problem faced by your prospect as soon as possible. They may not be fully aware of their problem. If so, make it your goal to outline what will happen in the long run if they do nothing about it. For example, you could mention that competitors may be facing the same problem and have already begun working on a solution. This could allow competitors to catch up to them or overtake them. Competitors may have hired new talent to work on the problem and in doing so, they may have drained the talent pool, putting your prospect at a disadvantage. Find the right talking points. A little embellishment may be needed. But beware of doom and gloom scenarios which may be one step more than what is required.

Audience Attention

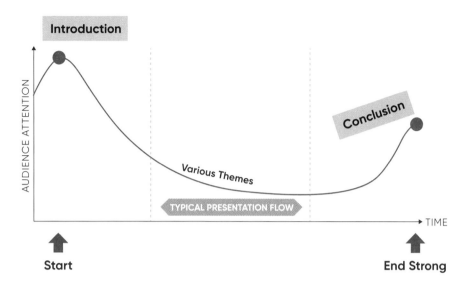

The ups, downs and ups again of the attention curve

The best salespeople are not in top consultancies or companies with billions in turnover, they are on the stage. Stand-up comedians (the good ones) can sell you the most difficult product of all: emotion. They make you laugh when they want you to laugh. They can laugh at you, and you even pay them to do it. What a treat for them! So, you have nothing to lose by using some of their tricks on your stage: your sales presentation.

Read this intro to a show by the comedian Michael McIntyre (Hello Wembley, 2009):

> *Good evening. Hello, Wembley! And how are you? Welcome to my show. It's Saturday night! Now, obviously, there would've been various reactions to your seats tonight. People at the back, thank you so much for being here tonight.*

They're miles away! Most of those people have sat down and gone: 'These are shit seats. They're shit seats. We probably should've just bought the DVD. It would be better just watching TV. Is that even him? I mean, it might not even be him. They could've just got any camp, Chinese man to run around. For all I know, that's Gok Wan.'

So, Wembley, my local gig - I've just come down the North Circular to be here. Strange road, the North Circular. People live on it. There are houses on the North Circular. Who lives on a dual carriageway? You never see anybody leaving their drive or entering their drive. I think if you move in, you die there because you can't get out. You have to go 40 miles an hour to exit your driveway. Can you imagine the tension every morning of your life? No, no! No, no. Now, go! You have to hope for traffic, then you can go out for the day. 'Fantastic news, darling - gridlock. Let's go out for lunch.'

McIntyre begins his story not about himself, but about ... his audience. It's all about you-you-you. Point two, he immediately addresses a problem: the bad seats at the back. One-half of the audience thinks: 'Indeed, we do have lousy seats.' The other half is relieved: 'Phew, I'm glad we have good seats.' Both groups immediately experience an emotion, McIntyre has demonstrated a common understanding with the audience. Et voilà: he has everyone's undivided attention.

But there is another thing we can learn from stand-up comedians. It is shown in this example: change direction, take sharp turns. Predictability kills attention. Building your pitch as a chronological narrative ('We started in 2018 and then we bought out X and last year we launched Y.') may make sense, but it is also boring. McIntyre switched nonchalantly from bad seats to houses along the motorway in Wembley, but it was done intentionally, for effect. Changing direction is a wake-up call, the loud finger snap that brings your listeners back to attention.

Audience Attention

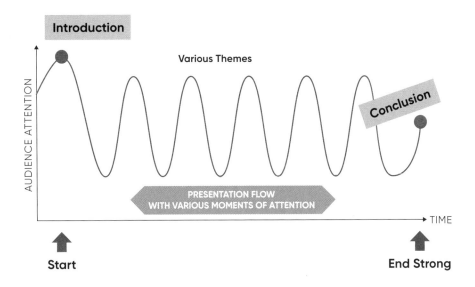

By incorporating elements of surprise into your pitches, you bring variation to the attention curve, create peaks (and sometimes deliberately valleys), and then round out the story at the end with a reference to the beginning. We do not like predictability, but neither do we like loose ends.

There is no need to take a course in stand-up comedy to get those spikes in your pitch. Here are a few handy techniques that take less effort.

- **Modulate your voice**

  This is basically a fancy way of recommending that you vary the tempo, volume and intonation of your voice when you present. Remember Fran Dresher, Miss Fine from *The Nanny*? Nasal, monotonous, slow. I get a headache just thinking about her.

- **...**

  Do not say anything for a while. Silence is powerful. When I have a room full of people in front of me and I notice that attention is waning, I stop in the middle of a sentence. Those who were zoned out for a moment think something is wrong, they refocus, and I can resume my presentation.

- **Whisper**

   Have you seen the episode of *The Office* where Daryl asks for a raise? You should. Regional manager Michael Scott printed out the top ten negotiating techniques from the internet, including speaking softly and used them to avoid giving in to Daryl. The best moment is when Scott lowered his voice to a whisper and said, so quietly as to be unintelligible, that a raise at that time was not possible. However, Scott spoke so silently that the ploy did not work. So, the content of his message was lost along with his credibility. But those 10 tips were pretty good, it is just a question of how he used them.

   Building in silence works. If you master the technique, you can hear a pin drop in the (meeting) room. Dosage is everything.

And now for the visuals: this is how to make them memorable

You need to be a grade-A, top-notch speaker to hold your audience's attention with your voice alone. This underlines the equal importance of directing and retaining their attention via your visuals. Despite their importance, slides are usually a) boring, b) ineffective, c) not attention-grabbing and d) all the above. Where does it go wrong, and how can visuals be better designed?

Two things that work in high school (and even then, it is doubtful) and nowhere else

When my 14-year-old son makes a presentation, he does this:

- Find cool pictures, blow them up (enter blurring) until the whole slide is filled, then strew unreadable text over them
- Bullet point the text, with each line having a different bullet point

Funny? Definitely. Replace 'my 14-year-old son' with 'the average sales rep'. Are you still laughing?

I see this not only in presentations but also websites and e-mails. So, are pictures and emojis forbidden? Yes. No exceptions. I explain why below.

Also, dearest son here is some free and totally unsolicited fatherly advice: learn to present your content visually so that people understand your message immediately. Read my section on causality. Or do not. Another thing. Learn blind typing. It will make your life so much easier. You will summarily dismiss my advice, but I love you anyway.

Background photos

You can use slide-sized images if they carry the right text. I like to have a few in my slide deck to emphasise key moments. Their impact can be great, and they can provide pleasant variety. But using them comes with a few conditions: the image must be powerful, contain contrast and work on the emotions. Plus, their timing in your presentation is key.

Your image must fit into the story and any text must be succinct and readable. Slide decks with only pictures do not do it for me. Sure, it is cool to present images without words. In fact, the visual impact can be almost overwhelming if you choose good images. But your audience will quickly lose the thread of your pitch. Another problem is that image-only presentations are not scalable because no one else in your sales team can tell your story in the same way as you. Another downside is that the slides will be unintelligible if you circulate them to prospects after your pitch. What do you forward to your prospects instead? A picture of a cup of coffee, followed by a blue sky and a grinning gorilla at the end? What are they supposed to remember from that?

Therefore, always combine your images with text. Ensure coherence: all slides should have a clear purpose, contain contrast and/or show causality.

Your current sales engine

1. Sales Process
2. How to scale & Grow (team)
3. Scaling Outreach strategies
4. Attractive Sales Content (BAIT) creation
5. Tooling

Time to grow into a CRO

Another thing: stay away from stock photos. Authenticity works. Images of your product, on the other hand, should be perfect. A good product photo inspires confidence.

Rocket, light bulb, thumb, poop

Aaah, emojis. Silent killers of the written word. Why craft good text when an aubergine says just as well?

Picture this slide:

… with our intelligent solution.

… according to this process.

… revenue increases.

I call this phenomenon icon diarrhoea. One word is not enough, it must be accompanied by an image. Tedious.

Icons are allowed, but if you ask me, there are rules. Use them in the following situations:

- For a process where you are displaying a unique approach. Keep them subtle.
- When they are unique and functional. They can provide recognisability and be part of your branding.
- In combination with your logo. For example, have your logo recur as a bullet point. If the use is thoughtful, this will come across as very intelligent and brand consistent.

Do not bet on being ready to create your own unique icons from the start. Get your storyline right first. That is your responsibility. After that, you may want to work with an agency that will get your design right. Certainly not a bad move because you can extend that design to your website, infographics, key slides you throw online and so on. When you are first starting out, consider using presentation templates. They are a blessing because they are inexpensive and give you rapid access to a beautiful presentation that is consistent in shapes, colours and fonts.

Six techniques to help you direct attention where you want it to go

People are visually oriented. If we are given text with accompanying images, we remember 65% of what we heard or read after three days. Omit the visuals this figure drops to 10%. (There is a reason why every company today has an animated video explaining exactly how their product works.) Do not make the mistake of underestimating the importance of visuals.

They underline your message at the right moments and make it stick better. We can manipulate images to increase their sticking power by using powerful and simple techniques. It baffles me that they are not used more often.

1. The red ball
2. Contrast
3. Powerful images
4. Arrows and lines
5. Movement
6. Causality and connection

I hear you thinking, 'We have a graphic designer for that, don't we?' Of course, but you have overall responsibility. You cannot leave the depiction of your raison d'être, your relevance, the heart and soul of your firm to the designers and the marketing team, can you? Thanks to designers, your presentation will be pretty, flashy, sleek or hip. But these aspects of your presentation will not convert prospects into customers. It is not the marketing team nor the designers who will be responsible for building your sales pitch. It is the person who meets with prospects, experiences their reactions and hears their problems who is responsible for that. In other words, you.

Do not get me wrong. Designers are vital. But in a corporate context, they are often trained to create uniformity. All slides are to be nicely aligned, with a picture and a logo in the same place, a design in keeping with the corporate identity, with a title for each slide, centred and at the top. Sounds sleek, but uniformity does not work for sales pitches. You need a slide deck that helps you to grab and hold an audience's attention, focuses them on your main message and leads to the Next Action and ultimately a sale.

My tip: The person who initially meets with prospects should build the sales pitch, supported by designers tasked with visually reinforcing the messages in the sales pitch.

1 The big red sphere

Visualise

80% of people are
visualy inclined...

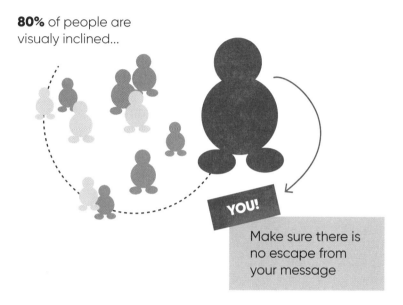

YOU!

Make sure there is
no escape from
your message

Picture this: a white slide, with a big red sphere in the middle, something you cannot overlook. Make sure your slides have an impact by including an object, be it an image or text, that is a real eye-catcher. Always combine text with a circle, colour area, image, etc. But be careful: the slide design should focus attention on only one object per slide. Spheres, plus fluorescence, plus a photo, plus a gif are just too much. No one thing will stand out. A tool that works well is to have one element recur regularly but in miniature. This is called the "recognition effect" and is a clever psychological trick to embed your message in the mind of your prospect. More on this later.

A big red sphere, with words: **your title**.

Visualise
your
message

Every slide should have a title. A title makes sure you cannot ignore what it is about. It is in your face.

Give each title a clear subtitle that immediately conveys the conclusion to be drawn from the slide. Again, the conclusion should be shown in a way that makes it impossible to ignore.

A word about conclusions: You might think it is best to let your audience come to the right conclusion themselves because you believe that will help them to remember it. Not true. It is up to you to make sure they cannot escape your message. Above all, you do not want to risk them missing your conclusion – the most important part of your presentation. Your job is to take them by the hand, to guide (lead) them through your story.

2 Contrast

Yin and yang, black and white, Justin Bieber and Mick Jagger: Contrast stands out, which is why it is one of my favourite techniques.

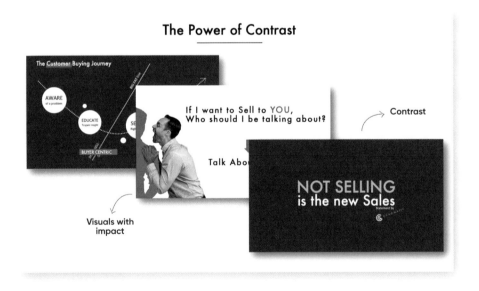

Contrast can be used as a tool to create impact for what you say ('small effort, big return') as well as for the layout of your visuals.

As I mentioned before, your prospects have changed. Have your sales techniques changed as well? When I talk about the future of sales in my lectures, I show an example of a sales pipeline with all its phases. As I explain the slide, the audience nods in agreement, because usually they are familiar with the concept of a pipeline. My next slide has one word:

STOP.

We are conditioned to stop what we are doing when we see the word stop, especially when it is written in capital letters (it captures our attention like the red sphere, remember?).

Check. With a slide containing one word, I have their attention. I say, 'This is not reality. This is a schedule. If you want sales to happen, you need to start thinking differently.' Next, I move to a white slide showing the solution to their sales problem. The contrast ensures that everyone's attention is focused 100% on the solution.

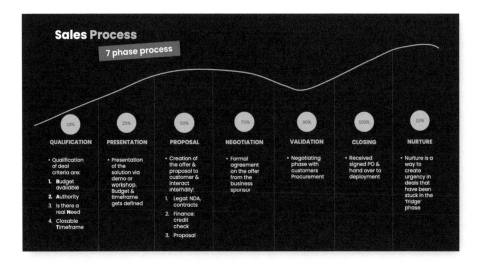

Contrast can be applied in a literal way by using contrasting background colours, for example. This is a simple and recognisable tool. Watch *Star Wars* tonight and see the ultimate contrast of good versus evil. That classic contrast is almost always depicted as black versus white. Princess Leia wears white, Darth Vader wears black. It is not only the Skywalkers that are depicted this way. It is seen as well in advertising, religion, classical painting, and in a wide range of settings.

I experiment with colour contrast by always placing the problem against a dark background and the solution on a white one. Or I use a dark image followed by a light one. This works particularly well to recapture the audience's attention. So, review your slides and add some contrast at points in your presentation where you want to be sure to have your audience's attention.

3 Powerful images

I am sitting in the audience. At the podium stands the next speaker who studies the origins of poverty. He lets one minute of silence pass before he begins.

'My name is X, but that is irrelevant. I am not here for myself. I am here for her.' A black-and-white picture of a little girl appears on the screen. In the background is a slum. She is sitting on the ground. An image so powerful that the whole room falls silent. It gives me goosebumps.

Salespeople are quite fond of pretty words, but sometimes forget the power of images. If images are used at all in presentations and pitches, they are usually clichéd stock photos or neat pack shots. Some presenters think images should be funny but ignore whether they convey the necessary messages. There is nothing wrong with humour, but it should be used in the right place. You do not want your prospects to remember a funny meme, you want them to be able to pass on how useful your product is.

Because remember: your listeners need to be able to relay your story smoothly and correctly. The decision-makers are usually not in your audience, but they are the ones you need to convince by proxy to get to your Next Action, which is the goal of your pitch. Therefore, use strong images that add value to your story and speak for themselves. Avoid images that are only gap fillers. A pitch is not an illustrated storybook.

4 Arrows and lines

When someone points at something, do you look at their finger or the object? (If you answered 'finger', you may put this book away and go do something else with your life.)

People like to follow arrows. It is so easy when someone shows us where to go. Traffic planners know this all too well and scribble arrows all over signs and roads.

And me? I like to experiment with my audience before I begin my presentations.

'I decide what you look at.' Rumbling and chuckling in the room. Three slides later: a white screen with a red arrow moving slowly from left to right, in sync with all the heads in the room. The arrow moves slowly across the screen. It stops. A caption appears: 'Told you so.'

Arrows are powerful tools to help you make your point, make connections and demonstrate causality. They also make your story a lot more dynamic.

- **Thick arrows** are used to make a strong point, to make connections.

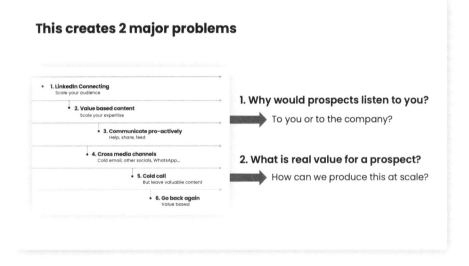

- **Fine arrows** are used for explanation and are great for explaining a product or showing how software works.

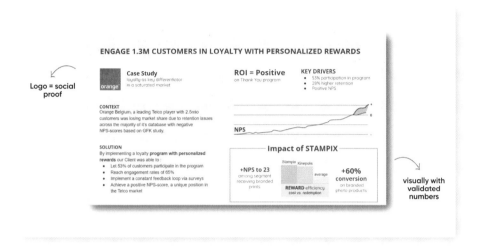

A special kind of arrow: the graph line

Growth, profit, margins and related values are usually depicted by line- or bar-graphs. As profits rise, the line or bars move upwards. Like arrows, we the poor sheep, are conditioned to follow lines. A line moving upwards must be good. It is no coincidence that many brands have an ascending line in their logos. Nike, Pepsi, and Adidas are a few examples

The same goes for the depiction of poor business performance. If I want to make the impact of a poor sales strategy very clear, rest assured that my line will plummet. There are always ups and downs, kinks and bumps in performance, so do not be overly concerned about showing this. It will help to make your presentation credible. So do not try to straighten your lines. Let them reflect the truth.

I must have given thousands of presentations and lessons over the last few years, so many that I have lost track of their number. Yet, apparently, this piece of advice stays with people. I am always meeting people who say, 'You're the man with the rising lines, aren't you?'

5 Movement

Standing still is going backwards, or worse: falling asleep. Go for movement in your slides. Move around yourself, too. Light, subtle movements are an efficient way to reinforce your words.

Movement in your slides
Use animated slides only to support communication of the most important messages and do so only sparingly to avoid diluting the power of this technique. Some suggestions on where to use movement:

- Social media: logos with slight automatic movement draw the viewer's attention. Also good on websites.
- Movement in your process: illustrate the use of your process by embedding subtle movement in each step as you progress through it. This will hold the attention of your audience.
- Cause-effect relationship: make an arrow move or pulse to demonstrate progression. Go easy on this one. This is not PowerPoint 1996.

TRANSITIONS (FLASHY OR OTHERWISE)

Speaking of PowerPoint. Ten years ago, I made a big impression with a presentation full of 'creative' transitions with cubes, swirls, and other objects flying around. It was unusable. Now I keep transitions between slides to an absolute minimum.

What I do recommend is to make the different elements (whether they are text, photos or processes) appear only when you click. This way, you keep control over what your audience sees. Therefore, never pitch using a presentation in Pdf format, but with a real presentation programme with the necessary features to activate animations selectively.

Can you also work with transitions if you draw on a blackboard, for example, during your presentation? Yes indeed. When I do that, I make one drawing per sheet. I divide larger pieces into parts, that way I get a logical whole and insure that the relationships between my drawings are right. In any case, if the audience photographs your slides or if they ask to keep a record of your scribbles you will know that your drawings made sense to them. Another point: Keep in mind that we read from left to right. Make use of this when you draw by starting schedules on the left side of the sheet, not somewhere in the middle. An extra tip: put your name or e-mail address on each slide in your deck. Make it easy for people to get in touch with you!

Move your body

Buy a pair of comfortable but stylish trainers and get moving. Get up and walk around during your presentations.

I was sitting in a board meeting. I completely disagreed with a comment that was made. The discussion was moving along so rapidly that it was impossible to voice my opinion. Fuelled by frustration, I stood up and walked around the table. I can assure you: this got the group's undivided attention.

Sometimes when I am with a client I cannot resist jumping straight up, striding to the screen and laying out my Sales Story from there. It is a great opportunity to direct their attention to where I want it to be. I can point to the screen and add momentum to the presentation. Admittedly, I often do this because I am easily distracted. Moving keeps my mind focused and it keeps my pedometer happy.

Movement can also be used to focus attention when making presentations on a stage. I back up my words with the right gestures at the right time. This brings an important quality, dynamism, to my presentation because the audience sees me in 3D. A lot has been written about the power of movement on a stage. We will stick to exploring how movement enhances conversion.

Movement on a sketchpad

Drawing is an old-school, hardcore, B2C technique. Once upon a time, for example, salespeople at the insurance company, Ergo, were trained to pull out a sheet of paper during their pitches and illustrate their prospect's need for insurance. They would first make a sketch of key milestones across the course of the prospect's lifeline. Next, they would superimpose an estimate of how the prospect's financial needs could evolve. These sketches prompted prospects to ask questions relative to the eventual purchase of a policy. (Personal connection, check!)

These sketches helped the salespeople maintain the prospect's attention. Ergo salespeople were able to illustrate the important and compelling financial risks that their prospects faced in the absence of insurance quite quickly and effectively. In other words, without Ergo, the all-important line we examined in an earlier section plummeted downwards. Ergo offered solutions that would make that line climb upwards. With Ergo all would be well. Blue skies ahead! That is the power of lines and drawings for your sales.

Should you buy a box of pencils and take a drawing course? No. But if you put something on paper, use a separate sheet for each concept you want to convey. Draw very simply and clearly. Sketches of processes with three to five steps work best, not too few steps and not too many. More on this in Chapter 6.

6 Causality and connection

All the above should lead to causality and connection. You want to make connections and links. Remember: you want your prospects to see the connection between their problem and your product.

Causality

The term causality refers to the connection between cause and effect, an essential element of sales. The first time I saw the power of causality in action was in Hotjar's visual shown below. Hotjar operates in the 'Software as a Service' market. This market evolves rapidly and is highly competitive, so quick conversions are essential. Players in this market test everything and continuously collect data, data that is also invaluable to us in sales.

The 'old way' appears on the left of the image and on the right is Hotjar's 'new method'. We already talked about contrast. Hotjar plays with the contrast between old and new in this image and they go one step further. They present the current situation as complex, sophisticated and muddled. This is communicated by using lots of arrows. They subtly add some dollar signs, whispering to you that the old way of working is also expensive. Their solution, on the other hand, is so simple and clear that it can almost be described without words.

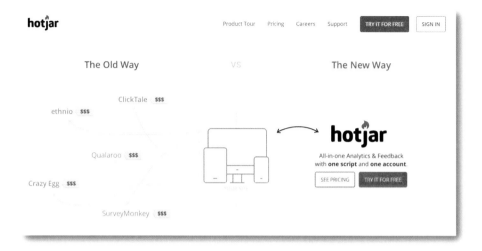

The effect of that cause-and-effect tool is magical. No explanation is needed: your listener's brain makes all the right links. From difficult to easy, from complicated to simple. From expensive to ... Even without reading the details, the message is immediately clear.

So never let it appear that you have a sophisticated solution. Or hi-tech. Or top-notch. That all sounds complex and expensive. No, your solution, however high-tech it may be, is simple and your visual representation should underline that.

Causality can also be used to magnify a problem. Consequently, the bigger the problem, the more useful your solution is. Show the problem and its impact on one slide.

Below is an example from Drift.com. Do not underestimate the impact of simple designs. Brilliant sales techniques have been used in this image: the contrast between old and new (nobody wants to be considered old or traditional) and the complexity of the old way's five steps versus the simplicity of Drift's solution are well illustrated. They also coined a new name for communicating with prospects and customers: conversational marketing. Attentive viewers will also spot the grey versus white background and the red versus green line. Brilliant in its simplicity.

Another great example of causality can be seen in the next image. On the left are a group of logos that prospects probably will not recognise. This is not a mistake. It is a deliberate strategy. The firms on the right side of the figure are doing well as demonstrated by the green bars. Except for the one red bar that the prospect will quickly see represents them (again, no coincidence). The slide shows that there is hope, that things can get better. In the next stage, the salesperson will explain how they can help to make things better.

Connection

Causality is one form of connection. You can represent it visually with arrows, but as shown previously, causality is usually implied by describing before-and-after situations. This works, so use this method. But there are a few more tricks that can help you make connections clear.

One is to connect different steps in a process. You show that they belong together and that the steps are in a logical order. Processes with a logical order are manageable and easy to remember. Arrows, lines, similar colours and shapes all help to illustrate connections. They make your slides more visually appealing, and they can help you to control your prospect's attention. Win-win-win.

In the following example, large and small spheres lead your eye to follow the arrows. You immediately see a coherent flow: easy on the mind and on the eye.

Which Customers do you want?

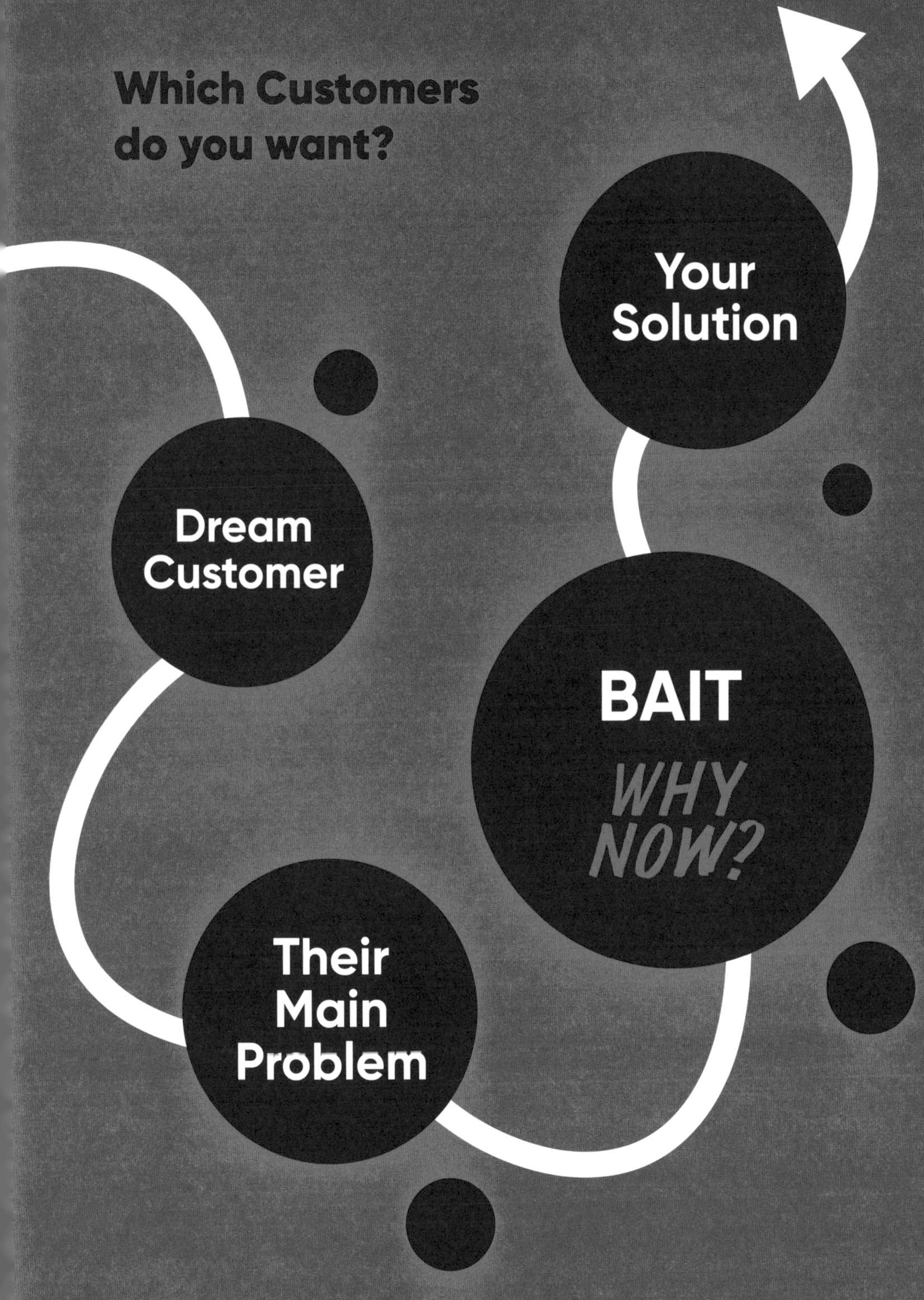

Your Solution

Dream Customer

BAIT
WHY NOW?

Their Main Problem

Go out with a BANG

What you better not do at the end (but what you have already done anyway):

- Say 'Thanks!'
- Ask 'Are there any questions?'
- Show a slide with your logo. (What? Seriously? A bit late, isn't it?)

I show a logo slide at the end of my presentations, and I say: 'Here is my logo. I love my logo slide.' My audience knows exactly what I mean: your logo does not say much about you, or your product and you cannot expect your prospects to be as in love with it as you are.

Attention is a remarkable beast. Billions have been spent on research into the how, the what and the why of attention. Because whoever can elicit attention has gold in their hands. In this chapter, you learned how to stimulate and direct attention.

We talked about the importance of the first few minutes, but you should not forget that the attention curve rises again at the end of your presentation. You can, you should, control this peak yourself.

You can do this very simply by announcing the end by saying: we are at the end of our presentation, two more slides to go, we are almost done, or the reception will start after two more slides.

By announcing the end, you trigger attention. This is because your listeners are expecting you to make them do something (ask questions, for example), or they suddenly realise they are hungry and there is a big, fresh, juicy sandwich waiting for them (also a positive emotion!). Whatever it is, they will be more alert than before. Make sure that your pitch truly ends within two to five minutes of the announcement.

In those few minutes when you again have their full attention, guide them to the next step. These final moments are critical. The message that you close with has been the overriding target of your presentation: your 'Structure' slide followed by the Next Actions.

I hear you thinking, 'My what? You mentioned Next Actions but what is a "Structure" slide?'

Don't panic, Chapters 4 and 5 are there to help you.

Finish it

I see it so often. Pitches with overworked intros, followed by some half-baked slides and ending with a hiss. If your prospect's initial response is 'Wow!' but their last one is 'Zzzz...' you are out of luck.

In one of my lectures, I tell the audience that, as salespeople, 'No' is one of the words they will hear most often. I say, 'Sales is like swimming in the lake of rejection', as I display a black and white photo of myself swimming in a lake (with clothes on, do not worry). A few slides later I close with, 'I offer a solution that will improve your conversion rates and have you sailing across that lake. You will have better conversion. Là voilà,' I say and show them a photo of myself sailing (in colour, still dressed). My story is complete.

As you close, make sure you can refer to one of your opening messages. Open-ended finishes make people uncomfortable. Complete the circle. It is like getting a surge of dopamine in the brain. It makes people happy and stimulates a spike in attention and this will make your messages more memorable

Having read this chapter, if you come back to me, enthused by how unique, ground-breaking and interesting your presentation has become, I will assume that it is. You have focused on attention. You have stimulated it and sustained it, visually and with words. Because if you fail to grab and hold your prospect's attention, you are nowhere. At best, attending your pitch will give them an excuse to ignore their administrative work or, at worst, it will be a distraction in a day that is already overloaded.

If you have mastered the tools of this chapter, you are now an accomplished guide who can lead the audience from slide to slide, from focal point to focal point. You play with red spheres, arrows, colour and contrast as if they were *Lego* blocks. Above all, you guide their attention like a blue route on a Google Map, leading your prospects to the next step, your Next Action. However, if your prospect has no current need for what you have to offer you will never meet the destination of Next Actions.

Through your Why Now you have proven that you are needed, or will be soon. To ensure that your prospect calls your number at that moment, you only need his trust. How you earn that, I'll tell you in the following chapter.

Proof with your Why Now that you are needed TODAY or tomorrow

CHAPTER 3

TRUST

No more slick talk: this is how you show your worth

If marketing is dealing in attention, then sales is dealing in trust.

'Michael, how do you build trust with your prospects?' Hardly anyone ever asks me this.

Strange, because surely trust is what a good salesperson should be working towards? Trust is the basis of every relationship: the one with your partner, with your mother-in-law and with your prospects. So why is nobody curious about the way to create trust? Do people think, 'Humph … not important?' Or perhaps people assume they have mastered that part of selling? I do not think that either is true. For example, just because someone once called you 'a born salesman' doesn't mean that it will be easy to win the confidence of your next prospect.

Plus, you also know by now that the classic sales techniques no longer work. Likewise, the stereotypes that went with them are fading too. Salespeople wear suits less often, the awards in the reception area are gathering dust, that pitch with a slide full of logos is vanishing and a slide with the number of employees and pictures of offices in Dubai or Shanghai does not cut it anymore. By now you know my unvarnished opinion on these things. They symbolise arrogance instead of trustworthiness these days. I am sincerely glad that the use of classic sales techniques is becoming less frequent and that the stereotypes that went with them are fading.

Trust is so essential that every salesperson needs to understand how it works. People like to buy, but they do not want to be sold anything. Being sold something can quickly feel like being 'sold out'. The line between the two is thin.

Trust takes time and expertise. How do you build a relationship of trust with someone you do not know (yet)? What techniques from the *Why Now Model* can you use to gain your prospect's trust? I will tell you all about that in a moment, trust me.

Social proof

Maybe you have one too, a slide with all your clients' logos; a hodgepodge of relevant and completely irrelevant (but familiar) ones, often crammed so close together that your audience does not know where to look first. Or even worse, you have two slides full of logos in your deck. Logo dumping is ubiquitous.

What are the messages behind this logomania? Do you expect everyone's mouths to fall open in amazement? Are you telling us something meaningful by drowning the audience in a sea of logos? Do you feel it is compulsory to show a logo slide that you rush over as quickly as you can? These are the messages received by your audience.

Social proof is powerful, this is true, and logos are one way to bring social proof into your pitch. But real people and real numbers will also bolster your words and engender trust in your listener. Unfortunately, techniques to convey trustworthiness are either underestimated or completely misused.

There are different ways to convey trustworthiness.

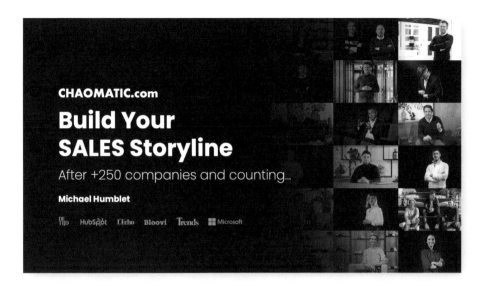

Faces

People trust people. People buy from people. Even chatbots are called Kate, James or Stephanie from Company X. Featuring people in your presentation gives it a familiar face. 'Humanisation' converts classic product-to-person sales into person-to-person sales. An evolution towards peer-to-peer sales is now taking hold, where customers recommend products to each other without the involvement of a salesperson. Focus on the person, not the product.

Show yourself, your staff and your customers. On social media, photos containing a person (preferably a child) still easily beat that perfectly styled bowl full of vegetables. So put plenty of emphasis on faces in your presentation, website and your landing page as well.

Wait, stop. Attractive and easy as it may seem, do not rush off to raid Shutterstock. Use photographs of real people from amongst your business relationships, even if the photos are somewhat amateurish. Nothing is more unattractive than photos of smiling, hyper-perfect people sitting in a meeting room, latte in hand apparently overjoyed to pass bundles of paper to one another.

In the real world, at least one person in each meeting is not paying attention. Show pictures taken in your meeting room, of your own people, even if one of them appears distracted. Nothing is more believable than - the wonderfully imperfect - reality.

I prefer to include faces at the start of my presentations and have them recur regularly throughout them, accompanied by a quote or an important insight. I end with a photo of the speaker's enthusiastic face, right next to the contact details. We remember faces better than words.

Follow Drift's example

Drift.com started as a chatbot but grew into a marketing platform. They have a deep understanding of the importance of using faces to elicit trust. They invented the brand-new category 'conversational marketing', which made them this category's de facto thought leader.

They also understood the power of faces. Their marketing material is full of them. Website, e-books, blogs, articles ... On every page, someone smiles at you. Very effective. Looking at a smile makes people smile.

Is that a bit over the top? Perhaps it is. But the gap between showing too many faces versus showing none is very wide. When in doubt: better too many faces than none.

Faces lead to clicks

We produce videos every day at Chaomatic. This includes thumbnail images for YouTube, Facebook, LinkedIn and others. Thumbnails are often used as a click target. YouTube and Facebook will generate thumbnails automatically if the user does not provide one. Do not depend on automatically generated thumbnails. Walk the extra mile and choose your own. We have noticed that people click through more often on thumbnails with a face on them.

Faces encourage feelings of trust, but the expression on the face matters. At Chaomatic, we ask people to make some crazy faces and use photos of them as thumbnails. After all, expressions stimulate emotions and emotions can lead to clicks. (And Mr Beast's too, for that matter, look it up.) We ask people to make some crazy faces and use them as thumbnails.

Using photos of people in presentations works for coaches, individual consultants, small firms and agencies. This may work for larger firms operating in some sectors where photos of people too but be aware not over perfecting them.

Quotes and other quirks

Google 'Elon Musk quote' and you will get about 89,000,000 results. Steve Jobs? About 47,900,00. You cannot compete with Apple's black slides with Steve's face next to his wise words.

You may wish to include an occasional quote on your slides. But caution is advised. A quote can make or break your credibility. Have you quoted Musk, as about 89,000,000 people before you have done? Then stop doing this now. It is like saying that Musk knows more about your business than you do. Quote yourself (although this is not everyone's cup of tea), quote customers, people in your own company or relevant and well-known players in your industry. This allows you to position yourself in parallel as a thought leader.

I use unrealistic or impractical quotes to create contrast, I just indicate that the quote is not realistic or practical. Or I give it a twist that makes me look like an expert. Another option is to include a triggering sentence, one that immediately stimulates the audience's attention and helps them remember the message.

Tip: always place inverted commas around your quotes. They attract attention and indicate clearly that you are quoting.

The title parade

Remember the maths-PhDs from the first chapter? Now is the time to wipe the dust off them. Not mentioning them at all in the company's presentation would be a waste of talent. On the other hand, showing off diplomas and titles too quickly can dampen attention. Using them at exactly the right moment – and subtly – helps to gain trust and credibility.

The Sales Story I created for a company that had developed a device to prevent lower back pain provides an example of the good use of titles. Their device was new to the market, so there was no way to add social proof and credibility to their Sales Story.

We applied some of the above techniques, but I became curious about the founder and sales director of the company who was very knowledgeable about back pain. I asked her how she gained her knowledge. It happened that she held a PhD in spinal anatomy. Found: the key to the company's credibility was the founder. We included her scientific credentials on the opening slide of the company's presentation and repeated them on the final slide with her contact details. Her background offered more credibility than her official title of sales director. That title put too much emphasis on sales and which we wanted to avoid.

The class photo

'Besides our headquarters in Brussels, we also have twenty-three branches worldwide. We just opened one in Tokyo. We have grown to ten thousand employees, so the cafeteria is full. Hahaha.'

Going on about the size of your team will frequently land you in hot water. Keep in mind that there will always be someone with more people and more offices. If you feel compelled to share this information, place it at the end of your presentation. If you show it only then, it means: 'We have experts in-house who can solve your problem local.' If you show it at the very beginning of your presentation, it won't have much more impact than a class picture.

If like many start-ups and scale-ups, you have real expertise in-house, then your team will certainly increase your credibility. But think carefully about how you present this. If there are only three in-house experts, you may put yourself in a weak position by mentioning this ('Is that it?').

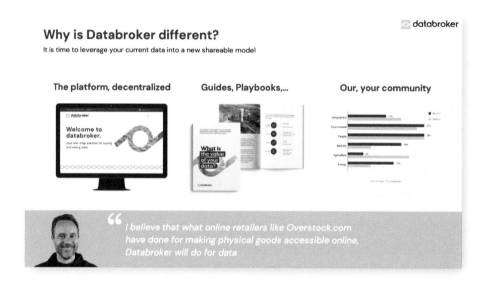

Keep in mind that not all pictures of smiling faces belong in your presentation. Recently, I saw a good picture of three guys on one bike. Cool vibe: they looked like cool guys to hang out with. But from the perspective of a prospect, would I hire them to advise on my sales strategy? Hmm. The credibility pendulum should not swing too far in the other direction either: leave out deeply sombre and serious photos where is not a smile to be seen. Feel free to have some zest in your photographs. Most importantly, your photos should exude strength and confidence.

The winning numbers

During a Sales Stories workshop at the company, Social Seeder, Patrick De Pauw, the founder, asked me: 'What kind of social proof should we put on our first slide?' Social Seeder offers a software platform that facilitates customer ambassadorship, meaning that people are the main social proof. But we pepped things up with an extra helping of validation and trust. Enter: the numbers.

Their platform has been accessed by 110,000 people. They could be proud of this number. It demonstrates that they are a rock-solid partner because if this many people use their platform, it must be good. So, we wrote, '+110,000 ambassadors trust us' on the first slide.

A similar story from a completely different industry. I advise a firm that generates and optimises spool files (the digital file sent to your printer when you click 'print') via a platform for large corporate networks. For them, system stability is key, along with the image that they can handle large production lots. After some searching, I learned that their platform had processed more than 1 billion spool files in recent years. This is a staggeringly large number, so we placed it prominently on the first slide. They instantly became a serious partner who knows what production and heavy duty mean and most importantly, this figure confirms that they can be trusted.

Another thing: do not faff about. 'We have between 1 and 10,000 customers' is not a lie if you have two customers. But is misrepresentation fair? There are many techniques like this that are used to disguise, conceal or exaggerate. Do not go down that road. You do not want to fall through the cracks and get a bad name. Make sure your figures are correct and that you can substantiate them. Otherwise, you are walking straight in the opposite direction from building confidence. It takes years to build up a good name, but one little lie can ruin it in no time.

Trust and numbers: it is all in the details

A charging station company showed me a slide that summarised their problem: 'Thirty per cent of cars don't make it to a charging station.' This was accompanied by a drawing showing 30% in large type and a picture of a charging station next to it. Not wrong, but rather basic. Different and better:

- Give exact figures. If it is 32%, write 32%. Rounding off gives the impression that you are manipulating the numbers. Be specific.
- Validate sources of quoted figures. Include the logo of the study agency or university that gathered the data. Place a '*' after the quoted figure and link that to a footnote. Or even better: show an intelligent graph emblazoned with the researchers' logo.

- Did you conduct the research yourself? Then make sure you speak with conviction to demonstrate that you are fully behind it. Although I respect the daredevils, be certain to have solid answers when prospects question your figures.

- Let someone else do the talking. For example, use screenshots of articles that mention your research. What also always works is to show an image of people posing a question that your solution can answer. 'Will I get to a suitable charging station in time?' can be a genuine concern. One that you can answer with your solution.

Numbers are powerful weapons, offering immediate validation and confidence. Whether you use the number of customers, transactions or partners, your prospect cannot ignore them. In other words, numbers are a very effective form of social validation.

Logos

Logos can be used in your presentation to gain a lot of credibility and trust. But remember the previous discussion about logomania? The use of logos should be a matter of quality, not quantity.

When I was vice president of a large software firm, we did not even talk about customers or prospects. We simply mentioned the number of logos we had gathered that quarter. If you get it right, logos work. They can validate the attractiveness of your solution immediately.

Which logos should you choose?

Choose your logos carefully. Make sure they are relevant to your prospect. Logos of clients always do well, but those with a media presence give your credibility an extra push in the right direction.

Logos are used to make a point or give extra legitimacy to your presentation. For example, I always use media clippings or statements to illustrate a market issue with the logo of the press agency attached. When referring to relevant studies, the logo of the research agency is also displayed.

How do you integrate your logos?

So logos are good, a 'logo overdose' is not. So spread out logos over your entire pitch. Use them as a backup for your statements and solutions. For example, it is not you who propose the solution, but the customer/newspaper/organisation behind the logo. That's a small operation that immediately takes care of an extra dose of trust and a strong Sales Story.

Feel free to start with a few references in the opening slide. With that, the tone is set. Subsequently, relevant logos will be placed in the places where youexplain exactly what your company does. The link between your company and the logos creates trust and credibility without having to say yourself that you have that.

Do not worry, everyone Is familiar with your logos. There is no need to point them out with your laser pointer or explain the link. Also, try to use companies' recognisable logos instead of names, when possible. Logos are more eye-catching than a list of company names.

Unless, of course, you have no visual support during your pitch. Then mention the names of selected companies, without making a long list of them (for example: 'Last week I was at … As we implemented it at X, Y and Z … Company X also had this problem and we … Currently we do a million transactions with customers like X and Y …'). Name-dropping, in other words. Without coming across as too boastful.

Back to your slide deck. I usually give all logos the same neutral colour. Everyone is equal before the law, and you will not distract too much attention from your sales pitch. Ultimately, the logos are just there to support your messages, they are not the stars of your slides. Colour or no colour? Compare the following examples and see how colour use affects attention.

Guerrilla techniques

I enjoy teaching and mentoring start-ups. Unfortunately, they are beset with trust issues. Or at least, when it comes to sales: no one realises (yet) that they have these issues (unless they have already read my book *Nobody Knows You*) and/or they barely have any customers.

There is only one thing to do, be bold. I recommend that beginners use guerrilla techniques. Three such techniques are:

1 Collect faces

Whether it is the face of a friend or an investor, this is the way to go. If you show only a face, without a quote, it does not matter who they are. They do not even have to be in the business. Their presence alone inspires confidence.

A start-up in AI asked me how they could make sure they were taken seriously. The solution: a slide showing a familiar face from the AI industry and an accompanying question. The next slide is the answer we developed. It illustrated a clear causality: listeners made their own link and we assumed they knew who that familiar face was. Is the relevance of that person's image meaningful? Then be honest about that (but only if they ask).

Michael Humblet

"How can we learn and improve **faster** on data-based relevance?"

The presentation and website had photos of customers with a quote explaining how they used the company's software.

It just works

The strobbo team thinks along and offers us great service and support.

LIESBET VERCAMER
BENELUX FOOD GROUP

Indispensable for profitability

An optimal planning is essential for the profitability of our company. Strobbo has become an indispensable tool in this.

OLIVIER DE BOLLE
TARTES DE FRANÇOISE

It's a must to report

Since the start of Strobbo, the discharge processing is a lot faster.

EVA URLINGS
BAVET

What does not work are inspirational quotes from notables like Buffet and Mandela. Set their quotes aside in lieu of quotes from people that are relevant to your audience, like bright minds from the industry or even brighter minds from your company. But no 'work hard, play hard' genre of quotes. You're building a Sales Story, not a Pinterest board.

2 Infiltrate the media

Actively seek your fifteen minutes of fame. Do not wait for the media to find you, make sure you are in the news or appear on a relevant website yourself.

Every industry has an established media outlet where everyone gets their information. Bloovi.be, for example, is a Belgian platform where entrepreneurs get insights on growth in the sector. Big firms buy screentime in the medium that suits them, but as a start-up you do not have that kind of money. What you do have are insights into something completely new. Bingo! That is exactly what news sites want. Make sure you produce content that the site can use immediately: the less work the editors have, the more likely your article will appear quickly. And make it as little about you as possible. Value prevails. Selling is not your goal here - or at least not immediately. What you want is to build trust and see your company's name in all the right places.

3 Get your logos via a shortcut

Your client portfolio may still be very light, but there are plenty of other ways to get logos that give you some extra credibility.

When I was just scaling my sales business, I put on my bold shoes and asked several top players in the sector like Bloovi, Hubspot and Microsoft on the (mostly) spot if I could create a video, article or webinar for them. Completely free of charge. People rarely say no when something is offered for free. My work appeared on their websites, and I was able to use their logos as a reference. A matter of scratching one another's backs.

Many start-ups build software or processes that are dependent on other software. The latter may already have a well-known logo. 'Compatible with Google' is a 100% legitimate way to attract attention and give yourself credibility. Even if you have not sat on the lap of Google's top brass, you just nicely linked Goggle to your product. It is a technique used by many SaaS start-ups and established companies.

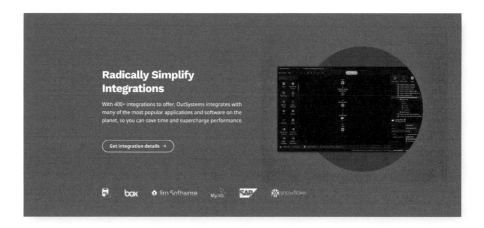

Finally, start-ups often work with an incubator like Belgium's Startit@kbc, Imec or The Birdhouse. You can use an incubator's logo if you are associated with one. Do you collaborate with a university for research? Add another logo.

There are options for sourcing logos, but do not take it too far. You do not want to jeopardise the relationship with a potential client by using their logo too creatively. Prospects quickly realise when they are being exploited, and this chapter is entitled 'Trust', remember?

Make the intangible tangible

A good loaf of bread sells itself. The look (that crust with a sprinkling of flour), the feel (crispy on the outside, buttery tender on the inside) and the smell (sweet, warm, just out of the oven) all play a part. But how do you sell something you cannot hold? Something that has no smell, colour or crispy crust. Services, software and everything in the cloud are intangible products. In sales, being intangible is a disadvantage.

The intangibility of the product sometimes delays the sales cycle. People tend not to trust something they cannot hold and tinker with: 'I will believe it when I see it.' If you do have a real product, it is always a good idea to bring it (or at least a part of it) to your meeting and literally put the quality on the table.

Touch it real good

Every disadvantage has its advantage. Just look at the example of Barco's ClickShare dongle. This is a small one-button device that projects your presentation (or anything on your PC screen) onto a larger screen via USB. Handy, yet prospects did not trust the thing at first. Why? The dongle was just too small. So much technology in such a small thing? Hmm. There was only one thing to do: make the dongle bigger and heavier. This literally made people feel like they had quality in their hands, resulting in good sales figures and a higher product price.

A scene from Jurassic Park explains it well

Donald Gennaro: [Tim pops up wearing a pair of night vision goggles]

Hey, where'd you find those?

Tim: In a box under my seat.

Donald Gennaro: Are they heavy?

Tim: Yeah.

Donald Gennaro: Then they're expensive, put 'em back.

Cloud software struggles with the same problem. The best example is Microsoft's Office365: finally, access everything from Office in one cloud licence. Ground-breaking, everyone would be happy, you would think. But some customers evidently prefer to dust off their PCs rather than use the cloud. Plus, they were used to getting something physical with that type of licence. Because sales of the online version of Office365 did not immediately take off, Microsoft put their new software in a box. They  made the intangible tangible. For the same reason, you can buy reload cards from Spotify, Amazon and consorts in the supermarket.

So how can you apply this concept to your Sales Story? Real boxes can help, but mock-ups will also get you a long way. The principle is the same: the intangible must become tangible. When it comes to software, I make things tangible with screenshots, preferably of the product in action. If you want to prove that your product also works on mobile, show it on a real smartphone or tablet.

An example is Wizata: AI software that automatically controls, monitors and improves processes. When I first saw their material, it was not immediately clear to me whether they were selling software or services, so I asked them, 'Which type of company do you want to be?' It turned out that they were prioritising software. It was clear to me: Wizata had to look like a software platform first and foremost.

How did we tackle that? With a beautiful image of their software representing a process. By putting lots of shadow behind it, we created depth and thus an impression of tangibility. We repeated these images in all transition slides.

The horn of plenty

The ability to make projects tangible is especially important for B2C marketing. When sales gurus sell you an intangible product like an online class or webinar, they often present it as a box, fan or booklet. This format offers them options. For example, they can stack the product to give the impression that you are getting a lot. They offer 'the lot' at a special price and look, the customer is sold.

In B2B, it is better to be more subtle. When we build online classes or content machines at Chaomatic, the designers know perfectly well what I mean when I ask them to, 'Make it rain content.' I want them to combine content in such a way that it creates an impression of excess. Lots of clients, lots of projects, lots of material. But how do we make the product look coherent and attractive?

We design sales storylines

If you're looking for a sales presentation, a sales pitch, a landing page for a marketing campaign, a mini-guide, canvas or a whitepaper, Chaomatic can design all these formats for you. Chaomatic is unique because of the blend between salespeople and in-house designers. So, you can be confident it will turn your prospects into buying customers.

Converting slide decks

The base of all sales conversations is a well-designed and attractive sales presentation (aka your sales deck). Chaomatic is a master in architecting the sales storyline so it converts. On top with our high-end design team we'll make it look very attractive so it can represent your brand properly.

The answer lies with Pinterest. Everything you save or post is conveniently displayed below and next to each other - a kind of content rain shower. I transported that grouping to our format and optimised the image with shadows to make it more tactile. By this means we combine videos, social media posts, blogs, downloads, online lessons and photos into one image with ease. Pleasant to look at and what you are selling suddenly becomes much more concrete.

Shadow and depth

Websites and presentations are often just a flat 2D mess: boring and un-attractive, and not good for the tangibility of your product. You can add depth to your images by using the following techniques.

I always give **screenshots** some shadow, as mentioned above. Shadows give objects a 3D quality and make them look more 'real'. This technique also works well for articles. Think carefully about what exactly you want to show. Screenshots of your software should be relevant, recognisable and logical. For your prospect, not for you. You know your software inside and out and will tend to show something that you think is cool or impressive, but it may not necessarily come across that way to others.

Which elements of your product should you show? Personally, I normally have two to three slides that cover the main features of the software. Because people like to have a sense of control, I always include a dashboard with graphs. It is the hidden features of your software that prospects ultimately spend their money on.

Folding corners creates the illusion of depth. Just look at the cover of this book. It suggests depth, but also the idea that you are getting access to a secret. Place a spot of colour, some text, a photo or an illustration behind such a corner to play on people's innate curiosity.

Hand-drawn flows and models. Speaking of folded corners, I saw a napkin amongst the classic sales brochures at a business event. Something was written in ink on one corner. Curious, right? I thought, 'Who knows, maybe I discovered someone's big secret.' I unfolded the napkin and found a complete model inside. I saw the person in charge casually putting these models everywhere. Brilliant. Such a trinket is a conversation starter, and it gives you the opportunity to explain your model. You say, 'Surely a napkin is a bit disrespectful?' This is about conversion and trust and you get those two in spades with this technique. It is such a great idea that I am now applying it myself.

(E-)books and white papers are deliberately presented at an angle on slides so that someone has to look twice to read the title. That way it sticks around longer. When you have an image of the brochure opened up, so that you already give away something of the inside. Every little bit helps to increase tangibility.

We build your B2B lead generating content machine

▶ For companies and experts who want to **scale their business** by leveraging **their own expertise** to generate **leads**

Be inspired   Contact us

Featured in:

Microsoft   HubSpot   HD   Bloovi   Trends

Fine lines.

I was in Paris. A mergers and acquisitions firm had asked me to tackle their Sales Story. Their slides at the time were very garish, with a prominent place for their own logo. I created a sleeker corporate look by placing a fine line at the bottom, accompanied by the logo (small and subtle) and the page number. The latter is especially useful for presentations that are also used in legal situations or are meant to serve as quotations. Such a line continues throughout the presentation as a kind of footer and it feels consistent and solid.

© *en TM*

You want to protect your intellectual property. A difficult balance, because on the one hand, you want to show off your unique methods and on the other hand, you do not want your prospect to adopt your idea or - the horror! - for it to leak to the competition.

In this case, it helps to add a - © (copyright) or TM (Trademark) symbol in small print everywhere, for example at the bottom of your fine line. This way, you subtly let it be known that you are not letting your feet or ownership be played with. Make sure you follow the correct procedures to protect your intellectual property. Where technically feasible and attractive financially, strategically and commercially, consider filing patent applications.

Consistency

Voilà, you have completed the chapter on trust. Check. Are you glad to be done with it? Do not be. Trust should be ingrained in everything you say and do. The above techniques will help you gain trust, but they are not sleight-of-hand tricks that you apply only once. Trust is a marathon, not a sprint.

True trust can only happen when there is consistency.

My classes on content engines and social media are invariably met with tons of enthusiasm. The course participants fly through the course in one day: they design, post, share, and like to the brim. But after a few weeks of using what they have learned, fatigue sets in. The level of response on their sites begins to dwindle and those hundreds of hoped-for leads do not materialise. So, I often hear back from them: 'Michael, it's not working.'

No, of course not, the effects are not eternal. All your friends, colleagues and uncle Danny fully supported you for the first few days and liked everything you posted. But they got tired of it. Moreover, they thought that after a while you no longer needed their help. The interesting audience - your potential customers – do not trust you yet or simply have not noticed you yet. Count on six to eight weeks before you start seeing movement, no matter how good your content is. And during those weeks, take the time to showcase yourself, for instance by responding to other people's content. That way, your prospect will see your name pass by a few times and you will be developing trust.

Designers are trained in consistency. Consistency creates calm and thus trust. This is precisely why, when first starting, you should not tinker with logos or colours. But as you read in Chapter 2, too much predictability is detrimental to your sales. At this point, the most important thing for you is to work on attracting attention.

Do not get me wrong. Although you have learned to vary your slides and to introduce surprises, you should not do this at the cost of calmness and consistency. Go for one style and reflect it in your whole slide deck. For example, stick to the same font and a recurring footer, and use the same filters for your photographs.

My first presentations and classes were visual chaos. I did not really see the problem until I outsourced the styling of my brand and slide deck to a designer. The resulting design became the basis for all my other materials. The professional look that the designer gave my presentation had an immediate effect on my audience The images stuck. The shapes were clear. Now the balance between consistency and surprise is a common thread in all my Sales Stories.

So herewith is a Humble(t) plea: if you need more ideas about how to build trust, ask me. Without trust, your product may be the best in the world, but no one will buy it.

What always works better than saying yourself how trustworthy you are, is having others say it. Building social proof is how you build trust. These kinds of techniques - plus patience, because remember that trust takes time - will take you much further than hollow words and vague sales promises. Trust is the basis of sales, the foundation on which your relationship is built and lasts.

Now good. What if your prospect trusts you, understands the problem and you have their undivided attention? Is the deal a sure thing? No! To achieve faster and more secure conversions, you need structure. If trust is the foundation of your house, then the structure is the logical layout that ensures you always end up in the right room. Time to start building.

Without trust, your product can be the best in the world, but nobody will buy it!

CHAPTER 4

STRUCTURE

Fit for a model: this is how you put your solution on the table

Structure: the key to conversions (and faster deals)

'**M**ichael, we have a problem closing deals. How do we make sure our deals don't get stuck along the way?' This must be just about the most frequently asked question. Or no, the most frequently asked question is 'Michael, is it actually Michael in Flemish or in English?' But closing comes a close second.

Suppose you have a good feeling about a prospect. You know they need your solution. The budget is there, you have approached the right people and sent a clear offer. You have checked all the boxes and your draft contract has been submitted. And still, no deal has been struck. Solid as a rock.

Usually, the problem is not with the famous closing, but with a previous phase. Selling is not: 'I am here with my product. Will you buy it? Yes/No.' The perception of prospects has changed and nowadays they can find information about their problem and possible solutions everywhere. So, you will have to offer value in a better way. You do this by gently guiding your prospect through your Sales Story towards your Next Action. Step by step. And if you do it right, you can sign the deal after four or five meetings. But everything that happens before the deal is signed is of equal importance.

Do deals fail because of problems with the closing technique? Sometimes they do. If you get lost in endless details and one more video, one more brochure and 'Next week we'll come again to explain how it works,' you are just delaying the final handshake. In these rare cases, a few closing techniques can help. In all other cases, the reason for deals getting stuck must lie at an earlier stage.

One possible reason: there is a problem with the *Why Now*. Either it is not clear enough for your prospect and he feels 'zero point zero' internal pressure to act. Or you planted the *Why Now* seed too late. When it does not work well, 'return to start'. In other words, reformulate your problem statement so that your prospect feels enough urgency to buy your solution.

Another possible reason: you have unconsciously created friction along the way, created barriers. Your solution is too complex, you have talked about yourself too much, or you used words like 'disruptive'. In this case, the problem lies with your structure. You need to build your Sales Story so that you smooth away any friction you may encounter along the way. Not just at the end, but in every slide, during every story and in every meeting.

In my CRM system, is a section I call 'the fridge', reserved for deals that have become frozen due to the wrong timing or friction.

How you ended up in the fridge

The CEO of a medium-sized company has seen your solution. During your meetings he nods, he is sincerely interested, the atmosphere is good, and he knows that the sooner he buys this product, the better.

Yet, nothing happens. He does not take a decision. Is it the price? No, the price is fine. Is it the team? No, the team is all set. Maybe they do not need us so badly after all? How can that be? Not only is their house ablaze: their floor has turned to lava. And yet, silence.

Recognisable? Not just for you. It is a daily occurrence for many salespeople. The cause: it takes time and effort to introduce your solution to a prospect. In a business under heavy pressure (read: any business), tackling a complex problem is ... complex. Many decision-makers simply do not have the bandwidth to grasp the problem and push your solution through quickly.

Suppose you have positioned your product with verve in a particular department. In most companies, your sales story must be communicated to other departments. 'Your deal is ready in sales, hooray! Ah, but wait, someone in marketing needs to look at it again. Uh ... that's not going to happen.' So, your deal remains somewhere on the corner of a desk, untouched. But that doesn't mean you cannot do anything about it.

Unburdening with structure

Fundamentally, your service or product is - forgive the ugly word - unburdening. You solve your customers' problems by taking away all their worries (about the problem you just threw on their table). But that solution must be simple: instantly understandable, clear, and recognisable. And above all: your Sales Story must be repeatable.

If you are standing there with complex new processes, product intros and different options, a whole firm needs to be mobilised to figure out whether it all fits their stall. Ain't nobody got time for that. Change is so tricky that it is often shelved. Change is so uncomfortable that it has been given a pseudonym: change management. You have heard of that.

Most business leaders are not eager for change. This is understandable. Change takes a lot of work, and it involves risk, not to mention the hidden costs in both time and money. Your solution is rarely truly 'plug and play'. Adjustments or integrations in existing technologies must be made as well as training, motivating and informing staff ... You can hardly blame company managers for feeling that the status quo is a good thing from time to time.

Salespeople get frustrated by this reality. Like cornered cats, their firms make the craziest leaps in product development - because surely therein lies the solution. But the solution does not lie in offering their product in a new colour or a new 'premium silver' subscription for their service. There is a more elegant and effective approach, one that needs to be applied from the very beginning of the Sales Story: structure.

Easy does it

The need for structure is obvious. You do not want your offer to end up in the drawer of dying vegetables at the bottom of the fridge.

Sounds tricky? Not necessarily. Because the biggest mistake is the easiest to solve. Most pitchers simply explain in too much detail what their product or service can do. Features, variations, extra possibilities ... information excess. If you put too many of those proverbial trees in their way, your prospect will not be able to see the woods.

So, STOP!

Think again. Think back to the beginning of your presentation. You started strong with two to three problems. How is your product going to solve those easily? Even if your seemingly simple solution is driven by hyper-complex AI that you are eager to tell them about, save the detail for another time, maybe. Your initial objective is to unburden your prospect, not overload them with super technical talk. Technology is something for you and your colleagues, internally. For the engineers and the IT people. Technology serves the solution; it is not there to make things needlessly complex. Later, by the way, there will be plenty of time to dig out all that high-tech in intimate tech circles. Your people talking to their people.

The exact inner workings of Google or Facebook algorithms do not attract advertisers. Far too complicated. But guaranteed: 'Thanks to us, your target audience will see an ad from you when they are in the vicinity of your shop.' Prospects are interested in the result, not in how your solution works. Keep this in mind as you build a very different Sales Story.

Repeat after me: my solution

- should fundamentally unburden my customer by taking away their problem.
- is a shortcut that can deliver more quickly than they could manage themselves.
- is tailored to the person sitting in front of me.

What I want to see in a presentation, or hear in a pitch, is how (and in what timeframe) your product or service will solve the problem. This will be presented simply and clearly, so it can be immediately understood and easily relayed within the prospect's organisation. The main purpose of your structure is to remove friction, scraping and sanding it until there is no excuse left for not implementing your solution.

An extremely positive side effect of a pared-down presentation structure is that it facilitates and can sometimes justify (or even increase) your price (your value). But the crowning glory and icing on your cake? With your ultimate structure slide, your model, you have a fundamental element to claim expertise or even thought leadership. But first, get your pitch right.

Six examples of rock-solid structure slides

Attention, time and effort are required when creating your structure slides. They will show how your service or product solves the prospect's problem, unburdens them, how your product works, and what your prospect can expect.

The positive impact of good structure slides only becomes clear when you see them in front of you. Here are examples from different sectors, from presentations with different objectives. There is one with a completely different approach and we even make a trip to the furniture shop.

In these examples, you will see how structure slides bring the elements I insisted upon earlier together: movement, arrows, working from small to big, the contrast between busy and quiet and how to use logos. Structure slides are so powerful that they make all the difference. I use them in every meeting and repeat them frequently. With structure, you whizz your prospect through your process. Zero friction.

1 The excellent model: Stampix

One way of putting everything into one slide is to make a model. This will not work for every type of product or service and your Sales Story can be coherent without it. But if it works - give it some time - your model can be your ultimate structure slide. It is the summary of how your solution works, the *raison d'être* of your product or service. Everything comes together in your model. When someone asks what you do, you pull out your model. This is just one reason why your model must be crystal clear. Simple. Immediately understood. I cannot stress its importance enough. Simplicity is so important that I devote a separate section to it below.

A good example is Stampix, a company specialising in customer engagement and brand loyalty. One of their products is a personalised photo service: people upload photos, Stampix prints them, puts a logo and a message on them and delivers them.

Time and again, Stampix's prospects underestimate how much work is involved in providing their services. It is just a photo and a simple process, right? Not if you want it to be done in a smoothly coordinated way throughout Europe with its language differences and various delivery modes and challenges. But their prospects do not see that.

Consequence: most prospects did not expect that they would need to pay a start-up fee (an entry fee to access the service), or they asked a lot of questions about it. They did not know what exactly they were paying for. A second issue was that existing customers did not understand the basis of the fees due if they opted to progress from a start-up relationship to a long-term contract. Stampix had failed to explain that smoothly. I was asked to help them smooth out these bumps in the road. As they presented their problem to me, I drew a timeline with key moments. They transformed that drawing into this gem of a model:

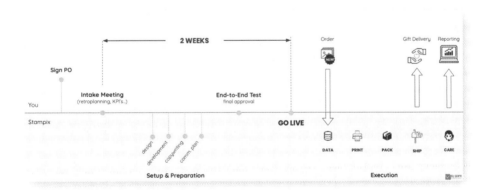

Why does this model work so well?

What immediately stands out are the two large sections: the customer in grey, Stampix in yellow. You see a timeline of actions: a few for the customer, many more for Stampix. The customer should appreciate the set-up work to be done by Stampix, but especially, how little needs to be done by the customer. This 'unburdening' of the customer is emphasised clearly by the design of the model: clear and not too busy. The world is already complex enough, your solution should be simple.

Pro tips
Make sure it is clear that:
1 Your client has barely any work to do
2 You do lots of work behind the scenes
3 The process is rapid: your timeline does not go on for years, it is quick and manageable

This structure slide now features in every Stampix sales call, right before they close, and it is reused in follow-on meetings. The slide is calming because it proves that the company has everything under control so that its customers can sleep well at night. Phew. The impact of this slide on Stampix's sales was huge: they closed deals faster, were able to increase their prices and extended existing contracts.

2 The model that saves time: Chaomatic

Practice what you preach, right? We also built structure slides and a model for our own business, Chaomatic. We offer companies the ultimate content shortcut. In one day, we record more than 20 videos that provide enough content to have a qualitative presence on social media for about six months. We offer a real content machine.

The reaction of every entrepreneur, when it comes to content creation: 'I absolutely get the point, but we just don't have time for that.' I use our model to make it clear that anyone can find one day of free time if the reward is six months of content.

Build the Machine: 6 months of content in 1 day

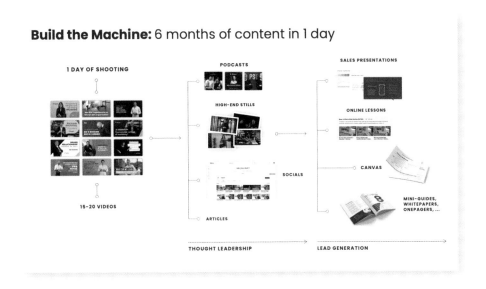

This structure slide brings calm to the busy heads of CEOs, marketers and decision-makers. It shows in black and white that our model works and that we and they can keep the process under control. Gone are friction and internal resistance. Our prospects are left with only one sensible reaction: go for it.

3 The model of a tight company: SettleMint

Remember SettleMint, the blockchain platform company from Chapter 1? I said then that they were way ahead of their time. The NFT and bitcoin world had yet to explode (and collapse again and explode again and …). You know the story. SettleMint had two problems:

1   They were just too early to market. For most prospects, blockchains were still plastic toys for two-year-olds. So SettleMint's pitches to B2B firms involved a huge amount of information, educational material and inspiration. In short: a lot of explanation.
2   Prospects did not trust the business. Who could put such crazy technology online in a few minutes? The disbelief was mainly amongst IT people who had already tried to build such systems. The IT teams were the group whose opinions SettleMint most wanted to change.

This structure slide was their salvation:

Our fast-track approach

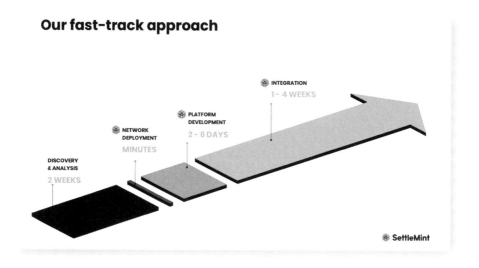

When SettleMint receives data from customers it is in a state of mumbo jumbo. Many companies think they are good at organising data, but this is not so. The first job SettleMint undertakes when they receive data is a big reorganisation: in their words, data integration. Then their platform is implemented - a few minutes work, so a very small block in the model - and the data is ready to carry on through the process.

SettleMint's structure slide is tight, clear and straightforward. I do not know how this slide could be more clear.

4 The model where it all comes together: consultancy

Most consultancies have structure slides in their presentations. After all, they are used to thinking in structures. The consultancy company in question here proves this point. Their business involves valuing companies and then selling them on behalf of the owners (often for more than the owners imagine they could realise). These transactions involve substantial sums of money and tough decision-making. Structure slides are particularly important in such cases. I have seen first-hand how the iron-clad slides shown below had a direct influence on major deals.

These consultants pitch themselves to prospects by explaining how they work and what they can achieve. They use a simple image consisting of three layers these consultants start with a simple image consisting of three layers.

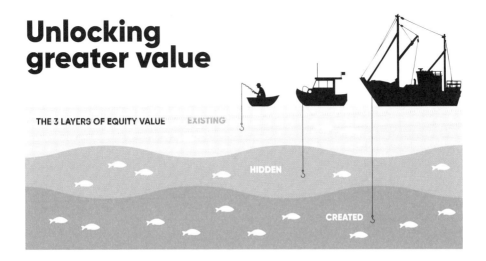

The above slide shows the three sources of value for their prospects:
1. The existing value: generated by the firms existing business
2. The hidden value: the consultant's estimate of the potential of the business present in products that have the potential to outperform those of the competition, untapped markets and untapped innovation in the business
3. The value created: the value derived from exploiting the untapped markets and innovations and product applications and/or combining the existing assets with those of an acquiring company. This sort of analysis is the big advantage of working with such consultants.

In the next slide, these consultants show their structure slide: a trademarked process in five steps. Together, these form a logical flow, indicated by the arrows and linked directly to a clear end.

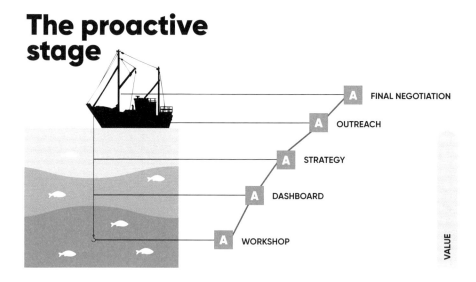

The proactive stage

A FINAL NEGOTIATION
A OUTREACH
A STRATEGY
A DASHBOARD
A WORKSHOP

VALUE

These images on their own make a big impact. But now comes the best part: a slide that shows, step by step, how the consultancy creates added value and growth and how they reduce anxiety for their clients.

Strong in all its subtlety. Note that:
- The slanted line heading upwards is not perfect
- The colours along the line change from light to dark
- The fine lines connect left to right
- The grey arrow highlights the growth of value

5 The model that helped land the job: Structure in your CV

Structure slides can also help you to sell yourself. A good friend of mine works in a top consulting firm. He was - quite rightly - offered the chance to become a partner. As part of the interview process, he was asked to give a presentation on himself.

Of course, a person does not become a partner overnight. They must demonstrate relevant experience, prove that they can deal with large clients, bring in new clients, fit into the team and show that there is sufficient growth in the segment in which they have expertise.

My friend laid out a timeline, depicted his accumulated expertise and indicated future growth in the market on one slide. He added recognisable logos, the relevant numbers and reflected all this in an ever-growing arrow across the slide. Here is his result:

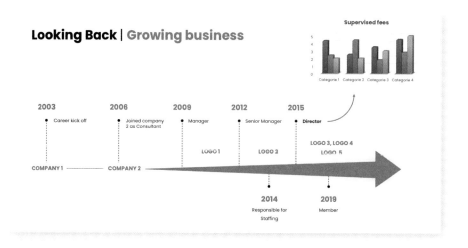

Naturally, he became a partner.

6 The model that made us buy a sunbed: **Structure and pricing**

Structure slides are also a handy tool for explaining prices. I had the chance to experience this myself one Sunday evening at about half past six.

'Michael, we have been invited to an exclusive garden furniture sale,' my wife informed me. 'Let me guess: black paper with gold lettering?' (Yep, I can still impress with my sales antennae.) Agreed. The next Sunday after-noon my wife and I headed for the garden furniture sale.

When we arrived in the car park, I noticed a saleswoman eyeing our car, probably to estimate our spending power. There was a typical friendly chat, we were offered a drink (cheers to reciprocity: the feeling that you should do something in return) and all our objections were expertly explained away (Selling on a Sunday? Selling at a special price?). This was followed by a tour of four showrooms full of furniture. As we entered one of the showrooms, she stopped at a sign to explain how her company operated.

TRADITIONAL

GARDEN FURNITURE CONCEPT

MANUFACTURER
AGENT
IMPORTER
DOOR-TO-DOOR
SALESMAN
WHOLESALER
DOOR-TO-DOOR
SALESMAN
STORE
CUSTOMER

MANUFACTURER

STORE
CUSTOMER

Structure slides: where, when and how

Where, when?

Sometimes I introduce structure slides at the very beginning of my presentation when I want to explain a flow. But without exception, a structure slide is needed at the end: make it clear how you will unburden your prospect. In this case, the perfect place to put your structure slide is right after you explain your solution.

Often, you will have shared some operational and tactical info at the beginning. Sometimes even a very small amount can be too much (at this point in the book you know that detail should be limited). When a prospect's limit has been exceeded you will see steam starting to come out of your prospects' ears. They will become defensive and look for reasons why your solution will not work for them. This is normal, you are suggesting that they change, and change takes effort, time and money. You will need to scour away the resulting friction with a structure slide. A structure can calm the minds of busy people.

And how?

My tip: start with the end.

Go straight to implementing your service or product. How do you install it? What steps are needed before the customer has a workable solution in place? How long does each step take?

You do not have to come up with answers to these questions on your own: enlist the help of the experts who will implement your solution. Those are the M/F/Xs who know the exact workings of your service or product. Extract from them all the info you need for a pared-down, crystal-clear structure slide.

Remember: the ultimate structure slide is not something you cobble together in a few days. Your structures, and certainly your model, need time to grow. At workshops on this subject, I ask all attendees to individually work out a structure slide – ideally, they should try to make a watertight model. This usually generates different points of view because, as with everything, the truth is always in the middle. One or two weeks later, they present their models. The results can be quite wonderful and can transform companies from within. So, take your time.

The following steps can provide guidance for the elaboration of your structure slides.

Step 1: Walk a line

The essence of your Sales Story should be condensed coherently into one line. If this is not possible then your Sales Story is too complex. The essence of expressing your Sales Story is that you can express it as a logical flow that can be understood immediately. In other words, you should be able to distil the whole process into one effective slide.

Step 2: Name the steps

Next, look at the individual steps in your process. Find a word that best describes each step or stage to give it a unique identity. By the way, structures with an odd number of steps have higher conversion rates and the content sticks better. No idea why, but it works!

Step 3: Close the loop

There are still thousands of people frustrated by *The Soprano's* open-ended final scene. We like resolution. Every good story has a clear beginning and end. The same goes for structure slides and certainly for your model. Return to the big problem your product or service solves. What is the cause-effect relationship between the problem (the cause) and its implementation (the consequence)? Usually, you need to tweak the problems a bit so that they match perfectly with the solution. Now is the time to craft a succinct and unique problem statement. This is where you complete the circle: you link the beginning to the end.

Step 4: Name your model

Did you construct a model? Then it needs to be given a name. Not only to ease communication but also to symbolise your expertise. If your name is on it, it belongs to you. Your model and the terms you use in it can give you a huge competitive advantage and position you as a thought leader. You will want your model to have a better name than 'Model 3.2 final'. After all, your model could become a household name. Just think of Simon Sinek's *Golden Circle*, Hubspot's *Smarketing* (Sales and Marketing), and Kate Raworth's *Donut Economy* or the *Food Pyrramid* by ... yes, by whom? Should your model carry the name of your company? You could do that. But if the focus of your company changes, the model's name may become awkward.

Step 5: Give your slides to a designer

Sometimes you cannot see the forest for the trees. It is normal to lose perspective, to become dug in. It can be difficult to climb out of your trench and review things from a distance. When I find myself in this position, even if my model is not perfect, I send my slides to a designer. They will not be aware of the details of the project and so will only rely on logic. When I see the result, I am stimulated to look at the slides with a fresh vision and can see the flow of my Sales Story reflected in the slides. Then I fine-tune the words or content a bit and make a final version.

Step 6: Test, test, test

Now all that remains is the testing phase. Not one test, but ten. Present your pitch to several prospects. It will take three or four run-throughs to master the presentation of your slides. You can then adjust your presentation and base your final structure slide on the highest common denominator in feedback. By this I mean, if 80% of your listeners notice the same thing, adjust it. There are exceptions: if people come up repeatedly with counterarguments to your logic or if there are points that are frequently misunderstood, then refining your slides may not be enough. You may need a different approach, such as customisation of your offer to include a premium service, for example. You could note this in your structure slide. Did you notice we are upselling? Once your foundation is firm and well-defined, sales conversions will follow.

The ultimate structure slide: your model

At the same point in every presentation, I see mobiles coming up to take pictures of the screen. If you were looking for feedback: this is it. Your listeners think your slide is worth saving for later, to pass on. You have hit a sensitive point. Either they think they are doing a good job because you are confirming their method, or you are offering a solution to a problem they recognise.

The most photographed slide? Your model. The three, five or seven (that is already a lot) steps which demonstrate in black and white that your solution provides the ultimate unburdening. Your slide that will give complex problems a simple solution. If your audience senses that they are stuck with that problem, they cannot resist the urge to take a picture or scribble busily in their notebooks.

> ### *Pro tip*
> *Structure slides, especially your model, can look great on your website and on social media. They can communicate a sense of order and calm and demonstrate your expertise. You can send your model to prospects, as a small gesture to support their decision-making, for example. This offers them great value and is a wonderful conversation starter. Or turn them into cool prints that you offer as downloads from your website. This is a convenient way to generate lots of leads in one fell swoop by collecting e-mail addresses.*

A well-designed implementation model, your ultimate structure slide, can be your most important asset. You will accelerate your deals with it and position yourself as a thought leader. Your model is your *raison d'être* and your actual intellectual property as a company. Believe me, your model is so important that you will want to print it out, frame it and hang it above your bed.

How cool would it be if prospects from your industry also had your model hanging on their wall as a 'Great Example'? Just be sure they call you when their house is on fire.

You already have a model

I was running a workshop at a major communications agency. They specialised in supporting product launches and activating whole communities around the launches.

After my explanation of sales models, I asked the participants: 'When you hire new salespeople, you give them a Sales Story. How do you approach that?' A long explanation followed. 'But now you literally sound like any other agency. Why do you win the big tenders and the others don't? Why do big brands trust you?' They responded with several reasons, but they could not give me a definitive answer. Even when I asked how they implemented their services, I got a far too detailed story.

I said: 'STOP. Shall I, even without knowing the details, try pitching your service?

If you want to build a brand like yours, you need to focus on three things. Step one is building content. But no matter how creative and cool your content is, you never know if it will catch on, so the response is unpredict-

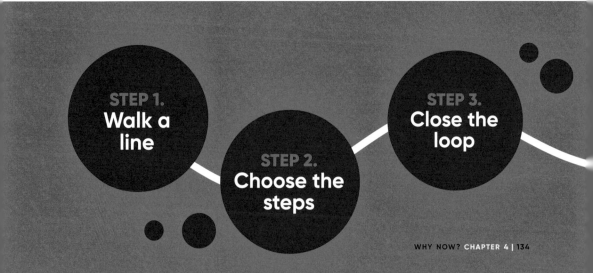

STEP 1.
Walk a line

STEP 2.
Choose the steps

STEP 3.
Close the loop

able. Step two is to build a community based on that content. That way, members (the buyers, that is) start creating content themselves, they make things come alive from within. The outcome will be more reliable, but it will still be unpredictable. Step three is to build your content and community into a culture. That way, you create the feeling that your product has a higher purpose, you will have much more impact and customers will begin to see your product as "the standard". You guys need to make sure you go from content to community to culture with those three steps.'

My words were met with silence.

'Michael, this makes so much sense! We can link our products to this and this and that and ... and ... and ... and ...'

My message completely clicked with them. The rest of the workshop was spent exploring how they could translate this model (which they therefore unconsciously already had) into a Sales Story, material for their website, and linked products and services. They admitted that they had been blind to their own business. As I have said before, this is completely normal. I too seem to overlook obviousness in my own business time and again. Sometimes you need someone from the outside to challenge you.

What helps me when I build such a model for someone else is that I have no in-depth knowledge of the business. I do not want to hear technical details,

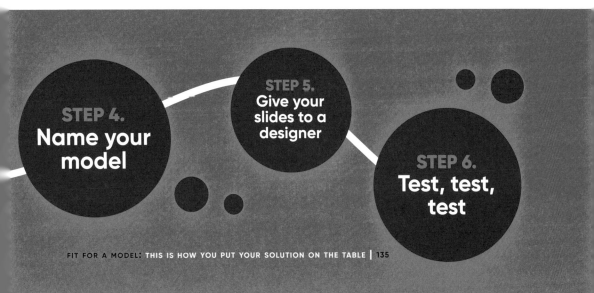

STEP 4.
Name your model

STEP 5.
Give your slides to a designer

STEP 6.
Test, test, test

for fear of getting distracted by them, or worse: fascinated. Then the Sales Story and the model would take a completely different turn and I just do not want that. A model is an ultimate abstraction and should therefore be as simple as possible.

How you build your model and integrate it into your Sales Story depends on a myriad of factors: what point you are targeting in the customer journey, the prospect sitting in front of you, the problem you aim to solve and even your personal identity. Let the examples in this book guide you, but do not let them limit you and stop you from developing your own vision. Keep it personal.

After all, your model is your base, your alpha, your foundation and your longevity. Or at least that of your business. Your model ensures that you stand head and shoulders above the rest: because you do something they cannot.

Effective structure slides will contain everything required by a good Sales Story: elements that drive attention, clarity that removes all possible counterarguments and friction from your prospect and an aura of confidence. Your structure slide shows the solution, and that solution must look super simple. A shortcut.

Structure slides serve as the capstone of your sales pitch. These are the slides that your prospect should remember, photograph and take to their meeting with the boss the next day.

Do you understand the usefulness and the how-to of your structure slides? Then you understand why a model - the ultimate structure slide - is such a value-add for any business. A strong model is like a stand-alone sales pitch. It is a promo, a system explanation, a who-are-we and your USPs all in one.

So never ask me about closing techniques again. Ask me about structure: it is structure and structure alone that will get your prospect smoothly from A to B, from no problem to Why Now, from no action to your Next Action.

And it is Michael in Dutch. You're welcome.

CHAPTER 5

NEXT ACTIONS

What's it gonna be: will you sell today or tomorrow?

'Say, Michael ...'

No, no. No more questions. This is the end of the pitch. Now come the words that make my hair stand on end: 'Thank you for listening to my presentation. Are there any questions?'

Sigh.

Was it agreed at some sales convention that we should end all our presentations like that? Then we wonder why it is that we have no impact, that by the last slide, our prospects have already forgotten what they listened to for the past hour.

What a waste, too. A waste of time. But above all: a waste of those last minutes of absolute attention. Why waste those golden moments on something that has no impact on your sales? Especially when you know you can control that attention if you apply the right techniques.

What follows is all you need to know about how to peak the attention of an audience, one last time. And, more importantly, to then turn that attention into forward momentum, into your future, into your Next Action. Nothing is more difficult in sales than turning words into action. In this chapter, we will look at how to make this happen and at techniques that work.

This is the end, my friend

You have come to the end of your pitch, the (almost) end of your Sales Story. From now on, your last slide, or your last words, will always be focused on action. Can we agree on that?

By now you know that you can find yourself facing your prospect at two points in time: either you are perfectly on time, or you are too early. You know how to estimate where you are on the timeline, but you cannot be completely sure. 'Urgency' is a subjective concept. Big companies have a very particular perception of time. For me, 'urgent' means something should have been done yesterday rather than today. In companies with complex hierarchies, a timeline of three months is considered rather urgent.

You do it and you do it fast

You need to know what your real value to your prospect is, to decide how to encourage them to take action. Knowing your value to a prospect is a fundamental requirement if you want to sell with foresight.

Your solution exists to take your prospect's mind off things, to unburden them of a problem. The customer trusts you to do things for them. Because you are an expert; because others have recommended you; because there really is no one else available; because they have no clue how to get started on finding a solution to their problem themselves. The latter is me when I call the plumber.

Important point: in most cases, your prospects can do what you can do. They just need to put a lot of energy and resources into it. No matter how unique you consider yourself and your talent, if Jeff Bezos wants to be able to do what your company can do, he will arrange it. And yet, he too buys products and services from others. Why?

Because Bezos - like your customers – does not want to worry about it. Secondly, you are a shortcut. You can do it much faster. Once they realise this, you are all set.

We need to pause at this point and talk about the Value Journey. Only briefly, I promise. The Value Journey is the path you take to build value to make a sale. The sale is the delivery phase of your Value Journey. You built your real value long before the delivery phase by inspiring and educating your customer. Your Value Journey is linked to the Buyer's Journey that your prospect follows:

- Either you are too early (no fire, at most a strange smell): then you will inspire and educate your customer (present problems, make the problem bigger, offer solutions) during your presentation, but also offer the content you created around it as Next Action.
- Or you are just in time (fire, fire everywhere!). Only then will your Next Action be a delivery action. Your prospect may order a custom-made demo, follow a workshop ... that sort of thing. But you do not propose a full offer for all your services straight away. That will come, but only at your customer's request, never the other way around.

The Value Journey Revisited

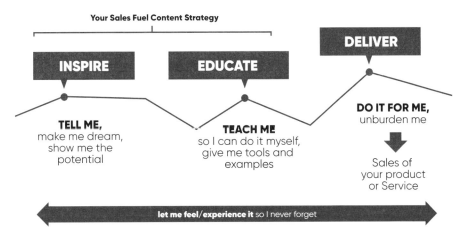

FIT FOR A MODEL: THIS IS HOW YOU PUT YOUR SOLUTION ON THE TABLE | 143

If you spend all your energy now on endless bleating about how your product works, and how good your company is ... then you only focus on fast delivery, on the 2.4% whose house is already on fire, who need your product immediately. Besides the fact that 2.4% is bitterly low, you have another problem: competition. You are fishing with a large group in that tiny pond. As a result, you will only be in contact with prospects at the very end of the sales cycle, when the prospect already knows exactly who and what he needs.

How do you overcome this? By getting back into the sales cycle. Like, way back. In an ideal situation even all the way to the beginning, so you can mould your prospects' perceptions to your model. This way, you create cause and effect yourself. There is only one realistic unwind and reliable shortcut: your company, your product and your expertise.

Inspiration

The first step is to inspire your prospect. A video on YouTube (or TikTok, these days), a book, a conference, a webinar, a whitepaper, an article in *Time* or racy words you plucked from the *Harvard Business Review*. Anything can be inspiring. Make sure you trigger inspiration, that you identify and stimulate your prospects' aspirations: this is what I want in the future, this is how we want to be, or this is how we are going to grow.

Not everyone in a company wants the same thing, so your pitch needs to be tailored to the aspirations of the different tiers of management and types of expertise. A founder may be most concerned with the future of their company: what direction should its growth take, do they want world domination, or do they want to sell the company and retire to their hammock in Hawaii within three years at a big profit? The employees will be most concerned with their own careers. How can they gain knowledge, develop their expertise, work their way up and get a raise? So, make sure you have a variety of seeds to plant so that inspiration can be found everywhere and for every kind of prospect.

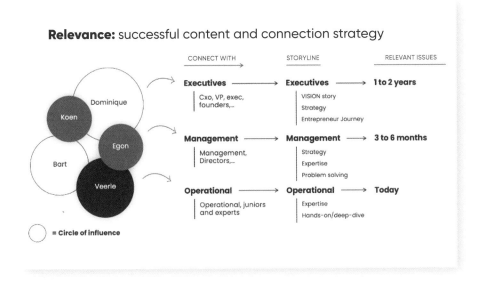

Relevance: successful content and connection strategy

CONNECT WITH	STORYLINE	RELEVANT ISSUES

Executives → Executives → 1 to 2 years

Cxo, VP, exec, founders,...

VISION story
Strategy
Entrepreneur Journey

Management → Management → 3 to 6 months

Management, Directors,...

Strategy
Expertise
Problem solving

Operational → Operational → Today

Operational, juniors and experts

Expertise
Hands-on/deep-dive

○ = Circle of influence

Education

Yes, the seed has been planted. You have inspired them. Now that they are all imbued with the vision of the future you offer them, you can sell. You show your product, you sit ready with a folder full of quotes to get signed … Alas. It was all a dream.

When you see that your prospect is inspired by what you are saying and you pull out your proposal just at that moment, nothing happens …

Nothing.

I have long wondered why this happens. The answer, when it finally dawned on me, should have been obvious. Take yourself as an example. What do you do when you discover something that inspires you? What do you think then? That you can do it yourself, of course. You are intelligent enough. Would you buy a product or service for something you can do yourself? I did not think so.

No, you would do your homework, read blogs and watch how-to videos so you could do it yourself. As a seller, you need to – skilfully – capitalise on this during the education phase. What if you were to provide your prospect with the material they would need to do it themselves? What if you fed your prospective customer useful content, with tips and tricks, insights, demos, and canvases, you name it?

You would be offering your prospect a lot of value, so this phase may take some time. Your prospect will need time to try and assimilate all the information you gave them. But that does not matter. If there is no internal pressure to act, they will not act. Whom do you suppose they will call the pressure appears, if their house catches fire, meaning when they are ready for the delivery phase? The expert of course. You.

'Yes but, Michael, is that really the case? If I tell them how to do it themselves, aren't they just going to do it themselves?' Well, no. What you cannot draw from a myriad of how-to blogs and instructional videos is experience or the speed with which you can do something that you have done many times before. This means that you are a shortcut for your prospect because you have a lot of expertise on the subject and because you can do it much faster than your prospect. The inspiration and education story is all about making your prospect feel that way. Rest assured: if that house is on fire, you will get a phone call.

Too early or on time? The choice is theirs.

Your prospect's exact location in the buyer's journey remains a guess to some extent. To avoid making a wrong guess, you need to address both options in your final slide. You will bet on two horses:

Option 1: You are too early. Then there is no point in pushing towards closure. Instead, offer your prospect two choices. Choice A: education in the form of webinars, mini-guides, white papers, surveys, online classes ... You name it. All this content is aimed at teaching your prospect how to solve their problem themselves, or at least provide valuable insights. Choice B: Inspire with case studies of how others have done it, keynote videos, events ...

Option 2: You are perfectly on time. You have landed in the middle of the 2.4% pond. To respond best to this, you need to be able to solve an immediate need, or even better: offer a shortcut. Your prospect wants a quick fix. It is up to you to deliver, in other words. What you want is to get to the Next Action.

You do not need to decide which option should be taken. That is a decision for your prospect. Throughout your pitch, keep repeating the two options. Just like in all your other communication, by the way. If during this process I explain the model, I make sure prospects can download it. If I discuss a case study, I make sure prospects can also get it online (education!). Giving options makes you come across as much less 'salesy' and builds trust. That freedom of choice is important, no one wants to feel drummed into a corner.

The choice should be most evident in your last slide. It will never again say – Thank you! Any Questions? See you next time! – or show a gif of a waving cat.

Your last slide will always give choices that prompt action. Because choices are freedom and freedom is priceless. You know the credo: 'Educate until they buy,' make that 'Activate until they buy.'

Next steps

Customised demo with the technical Experts on your Use case

Deep dive Use Case Inspiration session

Matthew Van Niekerk
Founder & CEO SettleMint

Keep it quiet

When I show that last slide with the various Next Actions, I deliberately say nothing about them. I do announce that we are just about done – a matter of having the focus back on – and leave that last slide there, like a big billboard shining in their faces. Showing that contrast between two options so clearly but not saying a word about it works. Every time.

Your prospects know well enough where they are in the decision-making process. By offering them choices, they will indicate which option they are interested in. If they choose the shortcut, then you know that your Next Action may also be the last step. Closing time! If they choose the education or inspiration option, then you will know you are too early. By choosing this, your prospect is saying *no* in a polite way, or *not yet*. This is your signal to take a step back and slow down.

Does there appear to be no internal pressure? So be it. Forcing such situations is pointless, even if you would use the most persuasive sales techniques. Yet, still, I find myself trying it sometimes. After 20 years of training in closing techniques, I simply cannot resist giving it a try every now and then. Look, no matter how you spin it: even if you can encourage them to say *yes*, that yes is usually premature and mainly a way of getting rid of you. You can follow up with them perfectly, but it is likely you will never hear from them again.

If there is no internal pressure, you must take it easy. You will need to establish a good relationship with your contacts and follow up with them – in a particularly low-key fashion – over the next few months until they smell smoke, that is until some internal pressure begins to build. Contact them every now and then but make sure you have a legitimate reason, such as giving them fresh, solid content. By working in a step-by-step fashion and adding content along the way, you will progress towards the Next Action and build up your value and trustworthiness in the process. With all your expertise and trust, your number is guaranteed to be at the top of their The International Conclave of Entrepreneurs (ICE) list.

What might those Next Actions be?

Your Next Action depends on how far along you are in your sales process. Are you coming to the end of your first meeting? Then your Next Action is to set a second meeting. See Chapter 6 for more on follow-up meetings and what you do and do not do at these meetings. If you know that the purpose of your next meeting is mainly to deepen your relationship with the prospect (get to know each other better and share more of your expertise), then your Next Action can also be something other than just a meeting.

Here are a few examples of Next Actions:
- Service/consulting business? Meet again to plan an analysis or workshop around one aspect of their problem. All are opportunities to demonstrate your knowledge.
- Software business? Meet them again with a customised demo. Suggest a technical deep dive (put the technical teams together). Offer free case studies, a webinar, mini-guides or a white paper.
- Product business? Plan a visit to show them your product in greater detail, consider a demonstration to make your product tangible or provide case studies from satisfied customers.
- Freelancer? Suggest a test. Use the foot in the door technique or conduct a short analysis that gives a tangible output in the form of a mini guide or a canvas.

These are only a few examples of reasons to meet again.

The offer

What do salespeople do when they are at a loss for words? Return to what they already know: the shortcuts. And what is the shortest shortcut in sales? 'I'll make you an offer right away.' Bam, in one straight line to sales and closing. With all the consequences: 'Yes, do. Just make an offer tonight after your dinner and the late-night news. I will then ignore it at my leisure tomorrow.'

The message Is submitting an offer should never be one of your two Next Actions. Ironically, an offer (quotation) simply contains too little value. That value is in your knowledge, your product and your software. That quote will come, but it must be at your prospect's request.

What can I do for you?

You offer your prospects interesting information and then you say, 'This is what my firm and I can do for you.' I see this in presentations, but also remarkably often in social selling. Then salespeople are surprised that their post generates little interaction or any response whatsoever. Remember: there is no selling in social selling.

Stating the obvious is of no use here. In fact, it is of no use anywhere. Why on earth would you conclude with what was already done and obvious? To make sure everyone understands you. Of course, you are the one who can help. The information you have just presented to your prospect demonstrates this. The only thing you achieve by submitting quotes prematurely is that you make the process longer and reduce your impact. So, stop doing this.

To sum up: are you too early with your solution? Then provide inspiration and education. Give prospects the feeling that they can do it themselves, but that you, with all your good advice and expertise, can do it much faster.

Your goal is always to get to the Next Action. In some cases, that will also effectively close the deal. A deal is the logical consequence of all your previous steps. Deal closings will feel very natural. That translates into satisfied customers and a full pipeline of even more satisfied prospective customers. What more could you want?

'This is the end of this Chapter 5. Thank you for reading. Are there any questions?'

Never again let your Next Action be to ask a question. From now on offer better and, above all, more and different options. There is an embarrassment of riches to choose from!

Now that you understand how attention works, you know how to create and use Structure slides and build trust. You created a non-negotiable *Why Now* mentality in your prospect and you know how to your prospects effortlessly to two possible Next Actions. Top.

Everything in the blender, mix well and done? It is not that easy. Just because all the elements are present does not mean they work. For that, they must move logically from one step to the next, interact and form a flowing whole. In short: you pour them into an ultimate flow.

Now you have two choices: either watch the video (schoolofsales.com/why-now?) on how best to apply your Next Actions. Or you can read further about how to build the ultimate flow.

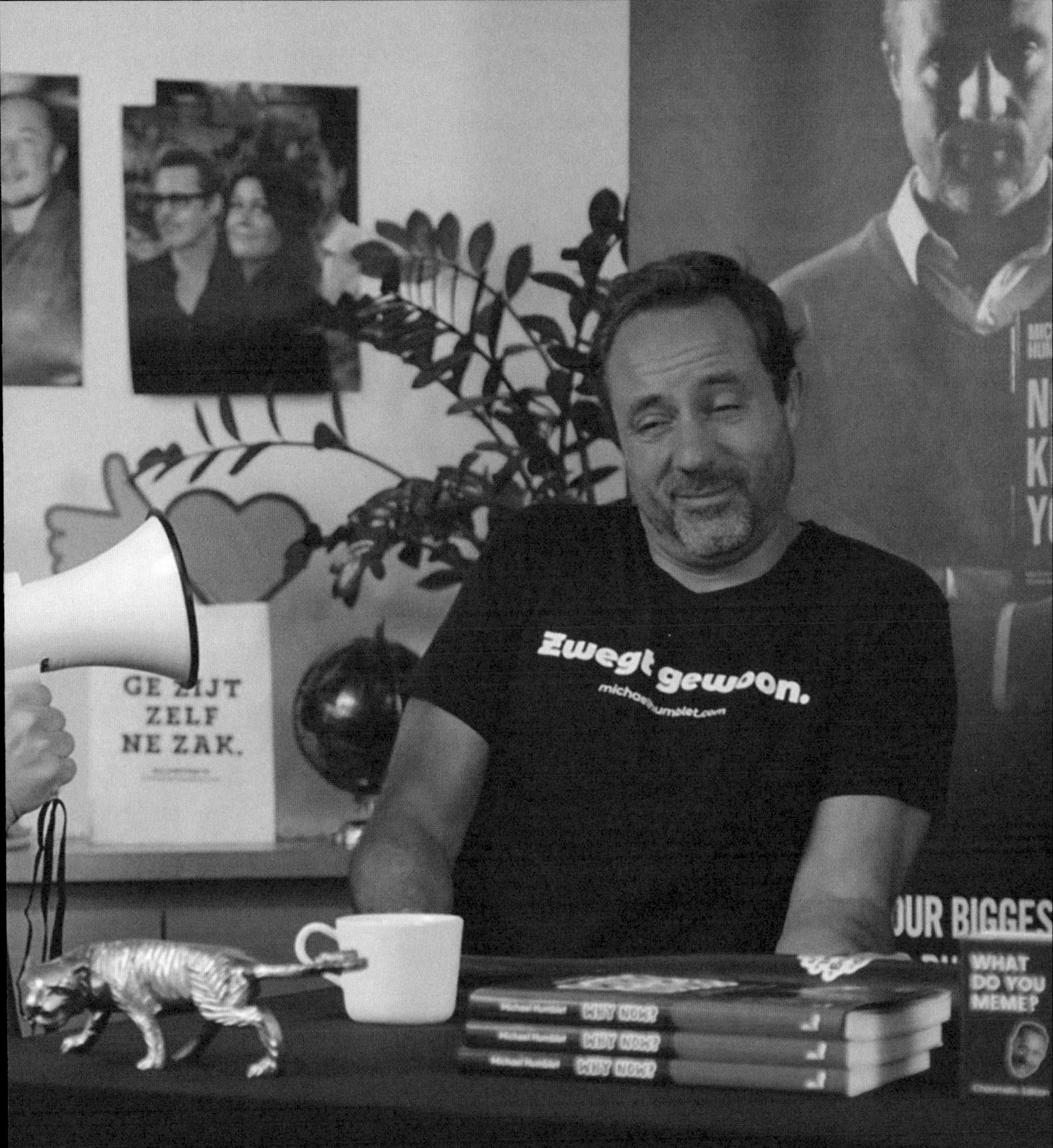
Zwegt gewoon.
GE ZIJT
ZELF
NE ZAK.
WHAT
DO YOU
MEME?

CHAPTER 6

ULTIMATE FLOW

Close (but no cigar): this is how you glue your Sales Story together

Your new mantra: Attention, Problem, Trust, Structure, Next Actions. These are the individual basic components of the *Why Now Model*. For each element, you can apply a host of sales techniques. These five elements relate to one another to form a sales process in which you bring all those components and techniques together into one logical flow. This is how you build an irresistible Sales Story, aimed at your goal: action.

The holy flow. There is no such thing. The optimum flow is situation-dependent. It depends on your sales technique, the stage your prospect is at and the people in your audience. The following paragraphs contain examples of a coherent flow or process that was developed within the context of a first meeting. An important bit of news: we are almost at the end of the book.

All about your Sales Story flow

Consultative Sales Story

The flow for consultative selling is fairly fail-proof. If you apply it properly, that is.

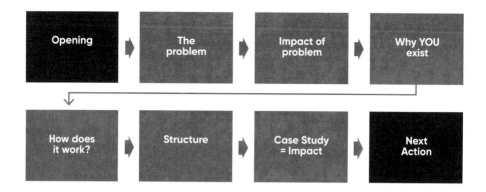

1. **The opening slide**
- one sentence summarising the impact of the solution (the end result)
- the name of the speaker
- social proof
- perhaps your logo (not necessary but companies like to see their logos, so I get it)
- an image of your product/screenshot of your software/render of your yet-to-be-built machine ...

2. **The problem slide**
- a clear cause-and-effect relationship that results in a problem, preferably structured in steps

3. **A slide about you**
- your sole reason for existence (to solve the problem from slide 2)
- the slide title should refer to the result that working with you would provide

- social proof
- two to three bullet points about the benefits of working with you from the perspective of the prospect

4. One to three slides on how your product or service works
- maximum of three slides
- or only one slide with your model
- if no explanation slides include a demo

5. Optional: a slide showing why you are different
- list two to three reasons
- the conclusion must be crystal clear so that it cannot be ignored

6. An impact slide
- a case study with figures

7. A structure slide
- one slide, no more
- summarise the implementation of your product in a number of key components
- social proof, if necessary, unpack your team and how it will solve the problem (works especially for consultancies).

Tip: you can combine your case study and structure slide: kill two birds with one stone.

8. Your final slide
- your two (always!) Next Actions
- your contact details (avoid using info@ ...)
- your photo - optional

Keep these two back-up slides in reserve:
- an alternative case study
- a pricing model

Provocative Sales Story

At first glance, this one looks like the consultative flow, but it is the little differences that, er, make the difference. Whereas in the consultative approach you move quickly to your solution (your structure slide, that is), in provocative selling you describe a black-and-white scenario, and you expose the negative consequence of not acting more dramatically, more bluntly.

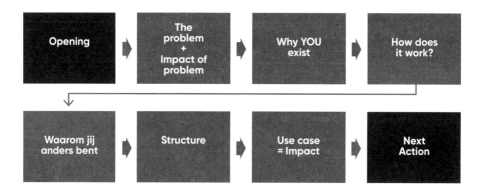

1. **Your opening slide**
- a sentence summarising the impact of the solution (the end result)
- the name of the speaker
- social proof
- perhaps your logo
- an image of your product or screenshot of your software or sketch of your yet-to-be-built machine

2. **The first problem slide (see the difference yet?)**
- two to three problems with a visual showing their impact or
- an image of something or someone that validates the problem like a publication, a published study, name of a well-known person

3. **The second problem slide**
- an expansion or worsening of the problem and a description of the consequence not solving the problem

4. A slide about you

- your sole reason for existence (to solve the problem from slides 2 and 3)
- slide title should refer to the result that working with you would provide
- social proof
- two to three bullet points about the benefits of working with you from the perspective of the prospect

5. One to three slides on how your product or service works

- maximum of three slides
- or only one slide with your model
- if no explanation slides include a demo

6. An impact slide

- a case study with figures

7. One or more structure slides

- one slide, no more
- summarise the implementation of your product in a number of key components
- social proof if necessary

  Tip: you can combine your case study and structure slide: kill two birds with one stone.

8. The final slide

- your two (always!) Next Actions
- your contact details (avoid using info@ ...)
- your photo - optional

Keep these three back-up slides in reserve:

- an alternative Case Study
- a pricing model
- a deeper understanding of the problem

Solution Sales Story

Solution selling is slightly more classic in approach. That is, you focus more on the solution than the problem. This is possible because solution selling is best for situations where your customer already knows very well what the problem is. So, what makes you special is how you will approach the problem - that determines your company's positioning. So above all, describe your problem-solving approach using your model as a guide. Preferably your model will demonstrate irrefutably your superior methodology for tackling problems.

1. The opening slide
- a sentence summarising the impact of the solution (the end result).
- the name of the speaker.
- social proof.
- possibly your logo.
- your logo, if necessary.

2. The first problem slide
- two to three problems with a visual showing their impact or.
- an image of something or someone that validates the problem like a publication, a published study, name of a well-known person.

3. The second problem slide
- describes an enlargement or deepening of the problem and the impact or consequence if you do not solve the problem quickly.

4. A slide about you
- your sole reason for existence (to solve the problem from slides 2 and 3).
- slide title should refer to the result that working with you would provide.
- social proof.
- two to three bullet points about the benefits of working with you from the perspective of the prospect.

5. A slide with the solution
- Your structure slide (show a model if you have one) as an overview.

6. One or more slides on how your product or service works

- maximum of three slides.
- or only one slide with your model.
- if no explanation slides include a demo.

7. One or more structure slides

- summarise the implementation of your product in several key components.
- your team will be important so introduce them and their skills and explain how they will help to solve the problem.
- social proof, if necessary.

8. An impact slide

- a case study with figures.

9. The final slide

- your two (always!) Next Actions.
- your contact details (avoid using info@ ...).
- your photo - optional.

KILL THE COMPETITION WITH CONTRAST

Whoever speaks about solution selling, speaks about competition. In your solution Sales Story, you can harness the power of contrast to eliminate the competition.

Imagine this sales situation. You pounce: 'The current sales training market has two problems: on the one hand, trainers without any experience and, on the other hand, training courses that focus too one-sidedly on one side of selling.' You smoothly come up with three possible solutions. And let those solutions be exactly what your competition is doing. Your prospects recognise this, they nod. Now create...

contrast.

You say, 'That's not going to work, is it? In reality ...' You describe your (far superior) version of the solution. This type of contrast showcases your deeper insight and proves your experience and knowledge of the market. And you have subtly exposed the competition.

Score!

All about your next appointment
How long should your first meeting be?

The first meeting should be short. Ideally, it should last about 20 minutes. That is too short to give (too) much information and just long enough to meet someone, get a feel for each other and establish a foundation of trust. Admittedly, such a short appointment takes some getting used to in an age where meetings are routinely booked for sixty minutes. Good, because it makes your meeting feel like a breath of fresh air (Phew! A relief!).

As you learned in Chapter 5, the next step after a first meeting is not necessarily a second meeting. Whatever that second meeting becomes, it can be a bit longer than your first meeting. It will give you the space to go into more depth. Your client will have the time to ask more questions, which in turn will show you what kind of meat you have in the frying pan. Raw, medium or already blackened by the flames?

Who and what is in the follow-up meetings?
Your follow-up meeting depends on the Next Action chosen by your prospect. Someone with decision-making power should attend. That may not have been the case in the first meeting, but now you really want to invest your time in a person with authority. Read: the person in charge of department X.

These are a few possibilities for the content of meeting two:
- You hold a technical deep dive. A meeting of up to an hour with the prospect's technicians.
- You give a customised demo to those who will be using your product (i.e. not the Procurement Department, but the CIO).
- You give a workshop. This can last from half an hour to two hours. Same here: the person responsible for the operatives should be at the table. You can bill your prospect for this workshop because you will be giving value right away.
- You hold a special case study meeting. You reveal deeper insights from the experience of other clients: information you do not share with just anyone. The management should be present for such a meeting.

At every meeting, regardless of type, you repeat some key elements:

- The problem (briefly)
- Your structure slide(s) (at every meeting). You are unburdening, you are a calming influence. Run through your structure slide at every meeting to detect any friction or sticking points, address them and carefully nullify any counterarguments.

What do you send after the meeting?

The meeting ended with a good feeling. As a follow-up, you send an e-mail with the full presentation attached. Right? I used to think so too. In my previous position - head of global sales at a big data company - we held sales meetings of up to two hours and then forwarded a presentation of eighty slides. Eighty! No one will ever open, let alone read, a file of that size. Except to revisit one slide: your budget.

> **See what they saw**
> How do you know which slides in your presentation are effectively viewed? Well, software like Hubspot and Qwilr will tell you. They tell you which slides were favourites, how often readers went back and how long they lingered on each slide. Handy, because if a prospect lingers on a slide, you can call to ask if there are any questions. These days, such functionality is often automatically built into CRM systems.

What do you send to prospects as a meeting follow-up? For that, you need to know where your e-mail will initially land.

Send a maximum of four slides. Always in PDF.

- Your problem slide(s)
- Your structure slide(s)
- A solution slide
- Your Next Actions

Your goal is to elicit a response. For example, sometimes we do not send the vision describing slide, then we are guaranteed to get the question of where that slide was. That gives us the excuse to reconnect, build the relationship and trust further.

Consider the hierarchy

A firm is structured hierarchically. You know this but I will point it out to you anyway. Taken together, there are three main layers: executive, management and operational.

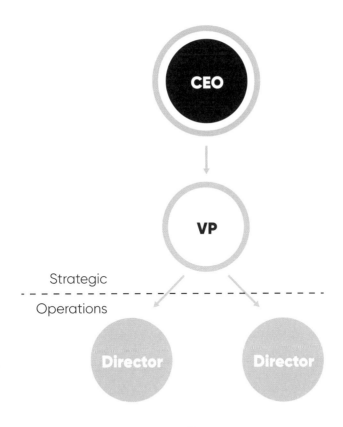

B2B Sales Process

All three layers have different goals and different problems to deal with. Your solution might unburden one layer, but the decision maker who decides if you will get the contract may be operating in another layer, with problems of their own.

For example: executives must seek board approval of budgets. Management in turn needs to go to the executives to explain the product. Management needs support from the operations staff to convince them of the usefulness of a product or service.

I take a shortcut: I immediately forward the material that the prospect in question needs to convince the others.

This is how to write an activating follow-up e-mail

That Next Action does not come out of the blue. Even if you have already agreed something verbally, there will be an e-mail in which you send slides and set the next date, no matter whether it is for a demo, deep dive or dinner with bells and whistles. For that e-mail, I will give you a few tips.

Keep it short

Your e-mail should not exceed a few sentences and end with two possible Next Actions. Long e-mails with long sentences and lots of questions are either not answered or you get a short yes or no answer. But which question exactly did your prospect answer?

So: a few short sentences (go to www.michaelhumblet.com/whynow for the best examples), a clear question (referring to your first action), focusing on the Next Action that your prospect indicated at the end of your pitch. The second action you subtly hide under your name. See next point.

B2B SALES-PROCES

Strategic

Operations

Execs care about:

- Top line revenue = Increase sales
- Bottom line = Cost reduction

Operations care about:

- Operational problems
- Solving short term issues

Talk their language:

- No details
- Strategic vision
- Show graphs/charts/ ROI numbers

Talk their language:

- Short term goals
- Help with operational problems
- Show real cases

Create sales material for their manager

To speed up closure and approval decissions

Go for a clear signature

Subtle is not: a declaration of love to yourself, like long, creative job titles, logos, prayer cards, contact details or logos of your socials ... Pfff. This goes wrong so often.

- Be careful with your logo and marketing banners. The e-mail programme often cuts these out and then your ritzy design becomes an ugly square. Nobody likes ugly squares.

- Super original job titles. Here is my track record: account manager, key account manager, sales manager, business development manager, sales director, buss dev director, EMEA sales manager, Vice President of Sales, Senior VP of sales, head of global sales, CRO (chief revenue officer) ... I understand the proliferation of titles. But what do they tell us? Often little, and in the case where there is 'sales' in your title, then often the wrong thing: your recipient immediately knows you need something from them. Whatever you do, do not end with 'sales representative manager chief officer president head'. A better idea is to summarise in one sentence what you can do for your prospect - something that is common on LinkedIn.

- Your contact details. Really? You would send me an e-mail with your e-mail address underneath? Then again, your phone number is a good idea, of course. Although I do leave that out in my standard e-mails. Beware. Most prospects expect action from you. When they call you, they are already in the middle of the blaze.

SO HOW TO DO IT?

Like this:

Michael Humblet
➤ **Your name**
Building your sales machine
➤ **Your impact, your value**
A sales technique to close every deal in 2022
➤ **The relevant Next Action, something educational and triggering (include a link to and e-book or video)**

You will have noted that your second action is there in your e-mail. It is hidden under your name. It can be there in the form of a link to a webinar, or a link to something that can be downloaded, or to an e-book ... If you also put tracking on the link (via bit.ly, for example) you can track who clicked where and when.

It's a wrap! Your Sales Story follows an ultimate flow in which you use all the techniques that work. Are you now going to sell everything and to everyone without fail, every time? I do not think so.

But you will sell more. I have seen it with my own eyes at the hundreds of companies where I have coached: their sales increased, relationships with their customers grew stronger and they converted faster.

Why Now is not a question. It is the answer.

CHAPTER 7

#JUSTASK
MICHAEL

Say Michael, and what about use cases?

ase studies give your story credibility. They show that your solution works and that you can be trusted. Even better, they speed up your sales process because they help increase internal pressure at the company. In other words, sharing your case studies is like pouring oil on the fire (the house should be on fire, remember?).

CEOs are often good salespeople because they have the experience to come up with lots of case studies to prove a point. This is a lot more difficult for new salespeople who lack specific experience. In this case, a list of references can help (the knowledge of the use cases).

Now then, let us look at how to use case studies in your sales pitches.

#justaskmichael
1. Where do I put a case study in my Sales Story?
Preferably towards the end, as a way of underlining what you have said and giving a final confidence boost, by demonstrating that what you have said works.

Equally, there can be merit in starting your presentation with a case study and using it as a problem statement. This gives you the chance to combine a few techniques, from social proof to showing expertise at the outset. You can present the outcome of the case study at the end of your talk. That way, you build up the tension nicely and have your audience along until the end. Full circle.

#justaskmichael
2. What if I don't have any references yet?
Tricky, but not insurmountable.

I was sitting in an office the size of an entire floor. Behind the desk was the CEO of a global telecommunications player. I had seen some impressive offices before, but his office was straight out of a movie. I thought, here is someone who values prestige. (Something you can cleverly capitalise on as a salesperson. Vanity is my favourite sin.) I also thought, 'I need to charge more for my product.'

Once we got started, I realised that the whole 20 minutes of the meeting – to talk about the impact of big data on their revenue – could have been spent discussing big data. That was what the CEO was interested in most. I proposed that we would analyse their subscribers' data to create targeted, impactful campaigns to increase their sales. Twenty minutes was not much time, so I ignored the slides I brought along and drew my Sales Story directly on a whiteboard.

The CEO was very interested and wanted to decide immediately – totally in line with his proud demeanour. As I prepared to leave, he said,' Michael, since we are talking about a substantial budget, I must take this to our board of directors. Please send me a case study on one slide.'

Um, I did not have one. Because my product did not yet exist – we would build it custom for them. I said something about no precedents yet and specific solutions and so on to which he replied, 'Michael if you want the deal, send me a case study on one slide. You know what to do.' With those words, I was escorted out by his assistant.

Back in the office, there was only one thing to do: calculate. The five of us locked ourselves in our conference room to quantify what impact our product would have on their operations and how much that would save the company. Then we built in some safety margins for ourselves and poured all the data into one slide.

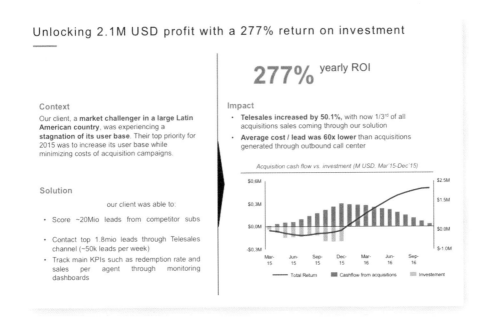

Unlocking 2.1M USD profit with a 277% return on investment

277% yearly ROI

Context

Our client, a **market challenger in a large Latin American country**, was experiencing a **stagnation of its user base**. Their top priority for 2015 was to increase its user base while minimizing costs of acquisition campaigns.

Solution

our client was able to:

- Score ~20Mio leads from competitor subs
- Contact top 1.8mio leads through Telesales channel (~50k leads per week)
- Track main KPIs such as redemption rate and sales per agent through monitoring dashboards

Impact

- **Telesales increased by 50.1%**, with now 1/3rd of all acquisitions sales coming through our solution
- **Average cost / lead was 60x lower** than acquisitions generated through outbound call center

Acquisition cash flow vs. investment (M USD, Mar'15-Dec'15)

I like to cite the example to dismiss all the excuses I hear, such as, 'Yes Michael but our product is not quite finished yet.' Sorry. If I can land a 750k deal with one slide of a product that does not even exist yet, then surely others should be able to do this with a product that is already on the market.

#justaskmichael

3. What if I am not allowed to mention the customer's name?

Maybe you have signed a Non-Disclosure Agreement with the client and they 'would prefer that you would not' mention them by name, or you have already asked six times if you may and have received no answer due to corporate unwieldiness.

Case 2: B2B Furniture 🪑
B2B Lead Gen

Customer

- Makes & Sells furniture
- Rep-driven sales organisation
- All fairs are cancelled due to COVID so looking for other ways to promote their offering

Wants

- Generate more awareness around brand
- More warm sales conversations
- Close new partnerships

Two options. One option is that in future contracts you reserve the right to use clients' names in case studies (bribe clients by giving some discount if necessary to be awarded this concession). A second option is to make your case studies anonymous. There are always ways to ensure that your audience can easily deduce which company is the subject of your case study. Everyone knows 'Belgium's biggest beer producer', as well as 'a Swedish furniture giant'. Upthrust, a growth marketing agency, uses this approach.

To prepare a one-slide or one-page case study, begin with the sector, then state in a few words what problem you are solving. On the left of the slide, provide a profile of the customer and on the right-side state what the customer wants. You will have shown the impact of what you propose to do. Clear. Done.

Success stories
FIND OUT HOW WE HELP OUR CUSTOMERS AND THE ROI GENERATED

LONG CARBON

- Sector:
- Market size:
- Main revenues:
- Eligible activities:
- Total number of employees:

MINING

- Sector:
- Market size:
- Main revenues:
- Eligible activities:
- Total number of employees:

LIMESTONE

- Sector:
- Market size:
- Main revenues:
- Eligible activities:
- Total number of employees:

4. But I have so many cases, which ones do I select?

I was asked this question by a company specialising in process optimisation for heavy industry. Think mining, for example. For them, it was difficult to choose the most relevant case study because their cases are so diverse. So why not capture that diversity in one image?

Two cases are more than enough for a Sales Story. Feel free to include more cases on your website, but in your Sales Story, you want to keep the focus sharp. If you notice during your pitch that the cases have traction, go in depth. Another good reason to have the real decision-makers at the table.

5. Say, Michael, when do you talk about money?

Sooner or later, someone wants to know how much it costs. The question is whether to answer, if so when, whether to give an exact price or a ballpark budget and how to put the financial picture onto a slide. Question by question, here we go.

6. Should you talk about the price?

Yes. If a prospect asks you what something costs, it is normal to answer. The big question is not whether you are going to quote a price, but when and how you will bring it up. After all, you also want to know whether what you are selling fits into your prospect's budget. If not, do not put any more time into it. If it does, take them to your Next Action.

7. When do you talk about price?

Definitely not in the beginning. You first want to understand your customer and understand their problem so that you can gauge what your product is worth to them. There are many studies that will tell you to talk about price in minute number 28 or 32. But those studies do not reflect who your prospect is and what stage you have reached in your Sales Story.

Think of the attention curve from Chapter 1, to have an idea of when I would recommend you bring up the budget.

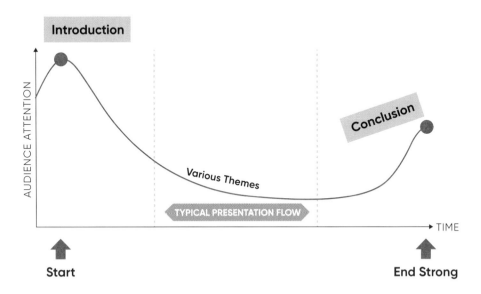

At the point labelled budget on the graph above situations where, you already have built some trust and credibility. This is the time to talk about the budget. If your first meeting lasts 30 minutes, bring up the budget at around 20-22 minutes into your talk. Rest assured that attention will spike as soon as you start talking about money.

With large projects and big budgets, this topic often comes up only in a later meeting. The first meeting is primarily used to sniff each other out. Usually, the decision maker will not be at the table. That comes later.

Situations will arise when you do not know if the budget will be discussed. Have a budget slide ready at the back of your deck, but only show it if someone raises the topic.

8. Do you present a budget or an exact price?

I made a mistake when discussing a budget in the early years of my career. I was selling software and services and had calculated exact prices, without knowing all the details and specifications. In the end, my prospect needed more than what we discussed at that first meeting. As a result, we went over budget. Result: my prospect felt cheated.

The lesson is that when selling services, you should make opportunities to talk about budgets and indications and price forks. Only if there are no variables involved can - the unit price of bananas, for instance - give you a concrete price. However, the price of bananas also depends on the weather, transport prices, etc. Anyway, budgets give an indication of the price, but budgets do not forecast the exact offer or the final price. So, play it safe.

9. How do you start talking about price?

Suppose you want to buy a car. In the garage, the top model is shiny and placed on a stage along with some fancy visuals. It looks so attractive that it seems your eyes are stuck to it. Posted next to the car is its price: too expensive for most mortals. What do you do? You look at the other cars for sale, more modest specimens, with prices that – in comparison – are not too bad.

This is called anchoring. You give your prospect an anchor point, a reference point of comparison and a departure point for the negotiation ahead.

You can establish your anchor point during your sales meeting. Start by asking a few questions to learn about your prospect's problem, how your prospect is dealing with it at present and so forth. This will quickly give you an idea of the magnitude of their budget. When the time comes - or you are asked - to talk about money, follow scenario 1.

SCENARIO 1

Storyline		Sales Technique
Customer X		Social proof: another relevant customer.
Had the following problems...		Bigger problems than prospect.
We found these solutions...		Confirm you can solve prospect's problems Structure slide shows process.
We found solutions for their bigger problems for around 50k (be vague).		Anchor the budget.

By mentioning those 'bigger problems', you build trust and show your prospects that you can grow with them. Pay close attention to their reaction. Do they continue to follow your presentation, or do they stop talking? Whatever you do, do not mention a lower price. If you do that you will be tied to that lower level. Are they showing indications that the price you quoted exceeds their budget (sighing, exchanging meaningful looks, rolling their eyes, physically backing away, weeping)? Do not panic. Scenario 2:

Storyline		Sales Technique
Customer Y		Social proof: another relevant customer.
Had the following problems...		Similar problems as prospect.
We found these solutions...		Confirm you can solve prospect's problems. Structure slide shows process.
We found solutions for their similar problems for around 30k (be vague).		The budget to suit them.

Social Proof (customer) + Problem + Solution + Budget

10. How do you show what it costs?

If your price is made up of several components, as with licensing models, you need to make the rates simple and immediately understandable. So do not discuss exceptions with prospects, base budget estimates on the services that 80% of your customers request. Any exceptions will be customisations and that simply will cost more.

In the SaaS (Software as a Service) world, they specialise in creating pricing models in the form of visual proposals. Type 'SaaS Pricing Example' into Google and you will find thousands of good examples. Incidentally, these are useful even if you are not in the software business.

In addition to this: four tips that always work.

1. Offer at least two choices
Most companies offer only one price. But anchoring works, remember? So, feel free to show two or even three prices. In SaaS, you often see three options, with the third being the custom option. The customer option is labelled, 'Price on demand. Contact us.'

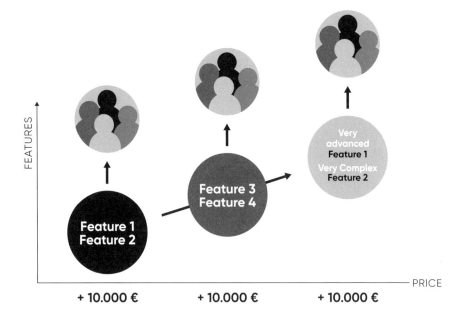

2. Keep it simple

Your slide should show only the essentials. The details should be presented in a formal offer or in a specific e-mail. Prospects can digest two or three more bits of information at this point, but not much more. If you start putting more on your slide it will become too complex. Complexity leads to friction, friction to delay and delay to procrastination.

3. Let attention peak

Use all the tips and tricks in this book. Play with colour, place the most expensive licence a bit higher than the cheaper option, display the options in tiers, and feel free to add a sphere with 'most bought'.

4. Use social proof techniques

Say you have three price categories. Then list a few small logos of references for each category. Very subtle, but this works well, as does a quote from a customer.

#justaskmichael

11. Should I give a discount?

As little as possible. You are sure of the value of what you provide, right? Then hold your ground.

A counter-reaction that I do occasionally enjoy using is the following: my prospect asks for a discount. I reply, 'No, I can't give a discount. But I can raise the price.' My prospect will gulp, but it makes them think twice about their question.

Everyone is looking for a good deal. So are you. In my experience, prospects appreciate it when you make a gesture. It does not have to be a discount, giving something extra will work too.

#justaskmichael

12. Say, Michael. What if I can't show slides?

You hold a roadshow (highly recommended) and it must be done by phone or at a networking event. No slides to hand? No problem.

Other frequently received questions and my answers:

The question I always get is: 'Michael, how can I do more deals?'
 ***This question strikes a note with most of my prospects.***

I reply, 'But that's not the right question.'
 ***Contrast***

I continue, 'This is an issue for 90% of my customers ...'
 ***Social Proof***

... but the problem lies somewhere else.'
 ***I demonstrate expertise and this begins to build trust.***

I share some expertise, providing value, 'Either they don't have enough leads in their sales machine.'
 ***FOMO. Incidentally, I deliberately used the words, 'sales machine', because I know this is what my prospect wants.***

Then I share a bit more expertise, 'Either their deals get stuck, or they don't go from A to Z fast enough.'
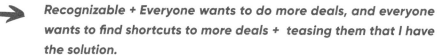 ***Recognizable + Everyone wants to do more deals, and everyone wants to find shortcuts to more deals + teasing them that I have the solution.***

In most cases, the prospect will start explaining their problems to me in the hope that I will solve them on the spot. That is the time for me to ask some questions so I know which case study might be relevant to them. The trick is to a) keep it short and b) give a concrete chunk of advice, something that makes them want more. If you get them to the next appointment, your conversion rate triples.

13. Say, Michael. How can I do that at a trade show?

Well, trade shows. You love them or you hate them. Getting conversion out of them is a challenge in any case. Everyone stands there in their conference booth at one of those high tables with identical material on it: a datasheet of the company, a brochure with the products and a plastic plant.

And after such a trade fair, there is always disappointment: 'How come our material didn't work? We had a Formula 1 car in our booth, didn't we? And we handed out customised cocktails, didn't we? We played virtual golf.' Cool enough and that certainly draws people. Just not the right ones.

Trade fair attendees aim for immediate conversions. But be aware: only 2.4% of trade fair visitors have an immediate need for your services. So of course, success rates are disappointing. What do you need to make a success of trade shows? Educational and inspirational material. Such as:

- Your Sales Story in a one-pager
- A booklet with your Sales Story and clear Next Actions
- A canvas example
- A mini guide

A deep tech firm had to go to trade fairs frequently, but they found the experience frustrating and wanted to do things differently. They asked me if there was a better way than the three of them standing around waiting for people to leaf through their brochures and then jump on them like hungry wolves.

I told them a story about some work I did a few years ago that I thought might help them. A company I worked with complained that they had too few meetings. I suggested that if one of their salespeople was abroad, they could call prospects and say, 'Hey, I'm in (say) Berlin on Tuesday, why don't I drop in?' It worked by creating a kind of opportunity tension, as in if you have come from so far away and are only here for a short time, of course, you are welcome! This approach was adopted by the sales team and salespeople began to fill their diaries with meetings.

Why not turn that principle around? Trade fair attendees want to use their time as efficiently as possible and be focused. The Sales Sprint principle works for such occasions.

A standard Sales Sprint goes like this: every six weeks, you go to one market in a very focused way. My choice of six weeks is not accidental: it normally takes five steps (one step a week for five weeks) before you can reach someone you do not know.

Apply that principle to a trade show and your sprint looks like this:

- You, the salesperson, compile a list of companies and people holding positions within those companies who are likely to be at the fair. Sometimes those details are listed on trade fair websites, otherwise, search on LinkedIn.
- The marketing and sales teams focus on preparing one new piece of 'bait', including a case study perhaps but above all something appealing, inspiring and educational. Read: not a sales brochure.
- The salesperson reaches out to selected individuals: 'Say, you are also going to fair X! Do you have time for ten minutes over a coffee?' Ten minutes is short and coffee is usually welcome.
- No immediate response? Then throw in the 'bait'. Otherwise, you save it for the trade fair itself.

That is how we did it. The '10-minute coffee' meetings had a huge effect on the company: 200 meetings at one trade fair. Another wave of meetings followed in response to the 'bait' the salespeople brought along and their good follow-up e-mails. You can imagine the impact on the bottom line.

#justaskmichael
14. Say, Michael. Can I really only talk about the customer? My product is so worthwhile.

No, you are not going to talk about yourself nor your product or service nor the history of your company or how many degrees your team has. Not until after 'the problem' has been defined.

The logic is this: because you use this time to demonstrate your ability to illuminate all aspects of their problem, you make your prospect feel that you also know how to solve it. This is something you want your prospect to feel. It is not something that you should need to tell them. You must be imbued with a desire to unburden your client and your client must sense this in everything you say. It is for this reason that at the beginning of your Sales Story you should only talk about your prospect and their problem.

This is how you make your customer feel that you are the 'Saviour':

1. **Your slide title should include the benefit your prospect would get by working with you**
   Example: 'Firm X is building a platform to give brokers administrative relief.' If that is the title of your slide, you are saying something about 'what', but not showing that you understand your audience's world. Better to write: 'We empower leading agencies.' The result is that you immediately solve the problem and sprinkle some FOMO, because what prospect does not want to be a 'leading agency'?

2. **Explain how you do it and why it is relevant to your prospect**
   Preferably with a few bullet points, but bullet points that are still not about you. So not:
   - we have the best technology
   - we have a patented system
   - our team of experts is always there for you
   The key is to turn it around. Not 'we, we, we', but 'them, them, them'. Focus on what is in it for them. So:
   - to accelerate your sales
   - to increase your margins by 5%
   - to empower your people with the latest information before your competitors

Illustrate a clear cause-and-effect relationship between the title and the rest of your slide. Result: power slides that are completely focused on your prospect and their context.

3. Provide proof

Time to show that you have already done this and are therefore credible. Social proof in the form of a few logos, you know the drill.

#justaskmichael

15. Say, Michael. What is the best way to talk about my product or service?

Situation 1: Your product can be held

In other words, your product is tangible: a machine, an object, something you can see and feel. A few tips for your slides:

- show the product with a crisp photo or a drawing
- use a drop shadow, it immediately makes images seem more real
- put your product centre stage, possibly with a brief explanation
- maximum three slides about your product

If you can, take your product or part of your product with you. If people can touch it, they will believe it. I once sold large document scanners. Too big to carry, so I only took the rollers with me: the piece that grips the paper. They were special specimens, custom designed and robustly built. I put them on the table halfway through my story. No one could resist rolling them about and by touching them they could immediately tell that the parts were made to last.

Situation 2: Your product cannot be held

You sell consulting, software, services, or something in the cloud. In this case, your model is even more important than it is for a physical product. Show your product or service in its context. If it is software, you can show it on a computer, for example. That can make what you are selling a bit more tangible. Add some arrows with minimal explanation and make an extra effort to make the slide self-explanatory. Let your model, or parts of it, recur in subsequent slides.

#justaskmichael

16. Say, Michael. Can I show a video of how my product works?

I have mixed feelings about demonstration videos. When I am in a meeting and I am shown a video, I wonder why I am not seeing the real product. Videos can be sent via e-mail, and you do not need a conference room to watch them.

Now, if you build AI-driven robot arms to put stuff on a conveyor belt one by one, it can be difficult to bring the whole of that setup to a first meeting. This becomes even more difficult if you have an international client base. The company, Pickit solved this challenge quite cleverly. They asked their customers, from Brussels to Rio, to send a box to their headquarters. These boxes were received and sorted robotically. Pickit streamed this process on YouTube. If you have a good idea AND make a video of it, show it in your sales pitch.

One more thing: if you show a video, it should be short and preferably focus on one aspect of the product or service.

I answered many more questions:

https://www.youtube.com/michaelhumblet

Have a question to add yourself?

Email me at schoolofsales.com/whynow
subject #justaskmichael

Outro

'Yes, but Michael, with us it's different. We are not like that. The way you present all that doesn't work with our audience.'

Uhuh.

I have heard that before.

Another excuse I get for bog-standard pitches is, 'That's how my manager taught me to pitch.' That is a fair point. I can believe this because I have been that manager who managed sales teams and gave that kind of advice. Advice that leads to boring Sales Stories and to slides that are more like a treatise than a model and focus on 'we' and not 'you'.

These were things that I learned from my managers and that they learned from their managers. The consequences of my sales choices when running my own company were much more tangible. I felt them in my own wallet. The fact that I was working for myself and not for someone else was also an advantage: I no longer followed someone else's rules. I could experiment and I developed an innate desire to keep polishing my sales pitch. When I got it right, I started doing the same for other companies.

My message is this: you do not need to listen to all those managers with their paint-by-numbers advice. There are other ways to sell. My approach to developing a Sales Story is simply one way that works, and it works well judging by the success of my clients. Enough of my social proof. My point is, above all: think for yourself. Act for yourself. It is your pitch. You have to land the deals. In the end, that only works if you put yourself into it.

Keep it Humble(t).
But always be yourself.

THANK YOU

Thank you

So many opinions, so many reactions, so many pictures and so many sighs. With that comes an equal number of thanks. Thank you to those who listened, to the event organisers who invited me as a speaker, to the incubators who let me loose on their start-ups and scale-ups, to the investors who trusted me, to the clients I get to work for every day with the wonderful Chaomatic team. I know, thanks are cheesy. But let me. Because without all these people, I would never have managed to bring structure and order to my chaos.

Thank you, Elke, my wife and personal coach on cover ideas who keeps me going ('crawl into your cubicle and get on with it!'). The one who keeps my two feet on the ground, like gravity, who keeps me humble with statements like, 'If you're not careful all these people will think that I hear only your whining.'

Thank you, Emma and Jill, copywriters who not only put structure into this story but also kept saying it could have 'even more Michael'. Let yourself go. It can be even wilder.' Always be yourselves, in other words. Thank you, Niels, my editor who persuaded me to write it today. Thank you to the proof-readers: Maarten, Elke, Mathias, Feline and Peter.

And thanks to all the people whose case studies, slides and stories I was allowed to use to create order out of chaos. Carl, Simon, Jan, Pieter, Dylan & Maarten (go go Usights), Philip, David, Wim, Loren, Joris, Andy, Raphael, Charles, Koen, Dominque, Matthew, Steven, Nick, Michael, Bruce, Kristof, Michel, Edward, Patrick, Frie, Alexander, Stef, Lorena, Kurt, Andy, Jo en Bart. There are a lot of you, so I'm going to possibly forget someone. But not really.

REFERENCES

References

Chapter 1

Dixon, M. & Adamson, B. (2011, 1st ed.). The Challenger Sale. Van Haren Publishing.

Van Belleghem, S. (2017). Customers the Day After Tomorrow. Lannoo.

Adamson, B., Dixon, M., Spenner, P. & Toman, N. (2015). The Challenger Customer. Van Haren Publishing.

Belfort, J. (2013). The Wolf of Wall Street. Adfo Books.

Mamet, D. (1984). Glengarry Glen Ross (Accessed 6 July 2022, from http://www.dailyscript.com/scripts/glengarry.html).

Gerencer, T. (2022, April 27). 200+ Sales Statistics [Cold Calling, Follow-up, Closing Rates] [Blog]. Zety (https://zety.com/blog/sales-statistics).

Gartner. (2019, September 16). Sales Development Metrics: Assessing Low Conversion Rates (Accessed 3 July 2022, from https://www.gartner.com/en/articles/sales-development-metrics-assessing-low-conversion-rates).

https://www.hubspot.com/resources/sales-reporting

Winning by Design (2022, June 29). Winning by Design | Sales, Marketing & Customer Success Training (Accessed 12 July 2022, from https://winningbydesign.com/).

Van Der Kooij, V.J., Pizarro, F. & Winning by Design (2018, 2nd ed.). Blueprints for a SaaS Sales Organisation: How to Design, Build and Scale a Customer-Centric Sales Organisation (Sales Blueprints). CreateSpace Independent Publishing Platform.

Carnegie, D. (1981). How To Win Friends & Influence People. Simon & Schuster.

Chaomatic. (s.d.). We build your B2B content machine (Accessed 12 July 2022, from https://chaomatic.com/).

Humblet, M. (2020, 1st ed.). Nobody knows you. Die Keure.

Knowingo. (s.d.). Learning Platform For Employees. Knowingo.com (Accessed 12 July 2022, from https://knowingo.com/).

Settlemint. (s.d.). Blockchain innovation without barriers. Settlemint.Com (Accessed 12 July 2022, from https://www.settlemint.com/).

Sweepbright (s.d.). A new generation CRM for forward-looking real estate agencies. Sweepbright.Com (Accessed 12 July 2022, from https://www. sweepbright.com/).

Barco. (s.d.). Clickshare: Seamless wireless conferencing for small to medium-sized meeting and conference rooms. Barco.com (Accessed 12 July 2022, from https://www.barco.com/en/clickshare/wireless-conferencing/cx-30).

Chapter 2

Tversky, A. & Kahneman, D. (1974). Judgment under Uncertainty: Heuristics and Biases. Science, 185(4157),1124-1131 (https://doi.org/10.1126/science.185.4157.1124).

Kahneman, D. (2011). Thinking, fast and slow. Farrar, Straus and Giroux.

Rossi, A.F., Pessoa, L., Desimone, R. & Ungerleider, L.G. (2009). The prefrontal cortex and the executive control of attention. Experimental Brain Research, 192(3), 489-497 (https://doi.org/10.1007/s00221-008-1642-z).

Bradbury N.A. (2016). Attention span during lectures: 8 seconds, 10 minutes, or more? Advances in Physiology Education, 40(4), 509-513 (https://doi.org/10.1152/advan.00109.2016).

Ebbinghaus, H. (1913). Memory: A Contribution to Experimental Psychology. New York: Teacher's College, Columbia University (http://dx.doi.org/10.1037/10011-000).

Haugtvedt, C.P. & Wegener, D.T. (1994). Message order effects in persuasion: An attitude strength perspective. Journal of Consumer Research, 21(1), 205-218.

Lana, R.E. (1961). Familiarity and the order of presentation of persuasive communications. Journal of Abnormal and Social Psychology, 62(3), 573-577.

Kahneman, D. (2000). Evaluation by moments: Past and future. In: D. Kahneman & A. Tversky (Eds.), Choices, values, and frames (pp. 693-708). Cambridge University Press.

Kahneman, D., Fredrickson, B.L., Schreiber, C.A. & Redelmeier, D.A. (1993). When more pain is preferred to less: Adding a better end. Psychological Science, 4(6), 401-405.

Alaybek, B., Dalal, R.S., Fyffe, S., Aitken, J.A., Zhou, Y., Qu, X., Roman, A. & Baines, J.I. (2022). All's well that ends (and peaks) well? A meta-analysis of the peak-end rule and duration neglect. Organisational Behaviour and Human Decision Processes, 170, 104149 (https://doi.org/10.1016/j.obhdp.2022.104149).

Redelmeier, D.A., Katz, J. & Kahneman, D. (2003). Memories of colonoscopy: a randomized trial. Pain, 104(1-2), 187-194 (https://doi.org/10.1016/s0304-3959(03)00003-4).

Redelmeier, D.A. & Kahneman, D. (1996). Patients' memories of painful medical treatments: real-time and retrospective evaluations of two minimally invasive procedures. Pain, 66(1), 3-8 (https://doi.org/10.1016/0304-3959(96)02994-6).

Keysers, C. & Gazzola, V. (2014). Hebbian learning and predictive mirror neurons for actions, sensations and emotions. Philosophical Transactions of the Royal Society B: Biological Sciences, 369(1644), 20130175 (https://doi.org/10.1098/rstb.2013.0175).

Columbia University Irving Medical Center. (2020, July 13). Why are memories attached to emotions so strong? ScienceDaily (Retrieved July 11, 2022 from www.sciencedaily.com/releases/2020/07/200713144408.htm).

Kensinger, E.A., & Murray, B.D. (2012). Emotional Memory. Encyclopedia of the Sciences of Learning, 1128-1131 (https://doi.org/10.1007/978-1-4419-1428-6_1008).

Öhman, A., Flykt, A. & Esteves, F. (2001). Emotion drives attention: Detecting the snake in the grass. Journal of Experimental Psychology: General, 130(3), 466-478 (https://doi.org/10.1037/0096-3445.130.3.466).

Tyng, C.M., Amin, H.U., Saad, M. & Malik, A.S. (2017). The Influences of Emotion on Learning and Memory. Frontiers in Psychology, 8, 1454 (https://doi.org/10.3389/fpsyg.2017.01454).

Cross, Z., Santamaria, A. & Kohler, M. (2018). Attention and Emotion-Enhanced Memory: A Systematic Review and Meta-Analysis of Behavioural and Neuroimaging Evidence (https://doi.org/10.1101/273920).

Kensinger E.A. (2009). Remembering the Details: Effects of Emotion. Emotion Review: Journal of the International Society for Research on Emotion, 1(2), 99-113 (https://doi.org/10.1177/1754073908100432).

Thorndike, E.L. (1920). A constant error in psychological ratings. Journal of
 Applied Psychology, 4(1), 25-29 (https://doi.org/10.1037/h0071663).

Talamas, S.N., Mavor, K.I. & Perrett, D.I. (2016). Blinded by Beauty: Attractiveness Bias and Accurate Perceptions of Academic Performance. PloS.
 ONE, 11(2), e0148284 (https://doi.org/10.1371/journal.pone.0148284).

McIntyre, M. (2010). Life and Laughing. Adfo Books.

Studio 42 (2009, November 16). Michael McIntyre 'Hello Wembley! [Video].
 Open Mic Productions (https://tv.apple.com/gb/movie/michael-mcin-
 tyre-hello-wembley/umc.cmc.6laltjs9n5s0iivtsbikrl9ua).

Wikipedia contributors (2022, July 10). Michael McIntyre. Wikipedia (Accessed 11 July 2022, from https://en.wikipedia.org/wiki/Michael_McIn-
 tyre).

Woodman, G.F. (2010). A brief introduction to the use of event-related po-
 tentials in studies of perception and attention. Attention, Perception &
 Psychophysics 72, 2031-2046 (https://doi.org/10.3758/BF03196680).

Childers, T.L. & Houston, M.J. (1984). Conditions for a Picture-Superiority
 Effect on Consumer Memory. Journal of Consumer Research, 11(2), 643-
 654 (https://www.jstor.org/stable/2488971).

Smethurst, S.E. (1953). Cicero and Roman Imperial Policy. Transactions and
 Proceedings of the American Philological Association, 84, 216 (https://
 doi.org/10.2307/283410).

Watson, J.S. (1860). Cicero, De Oratore, Book 2, 298-367. Attalus (Accessed
 11 July 2022, from http://www.attalus.org/old/deoratore2E.html).

Farrell, J. (1997). The Phenomenology of Memory in Roman Culture. The
 Classical Journal, 92(4), 373-383 (http://www.jstor.org/stable/3298408).

Soria Morillo, L.M., García, J.A.A., Gonzalez-Abril, L. & Ramirez, J.A.O. (2015).
 Advertising Liking Recognition Technique Applied to Neuromarketing by
 Using Low-Cost EEG Headset. Bioinformatics and Biomedical Engineer-
 ing, 701-709 (https://doi.org/10.1007/978-3-319-16480-9_68).

Raghunathan, R. (2012, January 17). Familiarity Breeds Enjoyment Why
 forced familiarity with novel experiences enhances enjoyment in life.
 Psychology Today (Accessed 9 July 2022, from https://www.psycholo-
 gytoday.com/us/blog/sapient-nature/201201/familiarity-breeds-en-
 joyment).

Mullin, S. (2021, January 27). The Science of Familiarity: How to Increase
 Conversions by Being Completely Unoriginal. CXL (Accessed 11 July

2022, from https://cxl.com/blog/science-of-familiarity/).

Mathy, F. & Feldman, J. (2012). What's magic about magic numbers? Chunking and data compression in short-term memory. Cognition, 122(3), 346-362 (https://doi.org/10.1016/j.cognition.2011.11.003).

Miller, G.A. (1956). The magic number seven, plus or minus two: some limits on our capacity for processing information. Psychological Review, 63(2), 81-97 (https://doi.org/10.1037/h0043158).

LaGesse, D. (2021, May 3). Putting a (Smiley) Face on Energy Savings. National Geographic Science (Accessed 8 July 2022, from https://www.nationalgeographic.com/science/article/100715-energy-smart-meter-competition).

Malaviya, S., Hernandez, M., Bhagavatula, K., Cibi, S., Ravichandran, K., Krishnan, S. & Jairaj, B. (22-2). Shifting Household Energy Use in Bangalore, India: Using Behaviorally Informed Energy Reports. WRI India and The Living Lab for Equitable Climate Action (https://doi.org/10.46830/wriwp.20.00046).

Osselaer, F. (2022, 8 January). The science behind how supermarkets tempt us: 'When you have a choice of three options, your alarm bells should go off.' De Morgen (Accessed 9 July 2022, from https://www.demorgen.be/voor-u-uitgelegd/de-wetenschap-achter-hoe-supermarkten-ons-verleiden-als-je-de-keuze-hebt-uit-drie-opties-dan-moeten-je-alarmbellen-afgaan~b115e268/).

Jeong, Y., Oh, S., Kang, Y. & Kim, S.H. (2021). Impacts of Visualizations on Decoy Effects. International Journal of Environmental Research and Public Health, 18(23), 12674 (https://doi.org/10.3390/ijerph182312674).

Chernev, A., Böckenholt, U. & Goodman, J. (2015). Choice overload: A conceptual review and meta-analysis. Journal of Consumer Psychology, 25(2), 333-358 (https://doi.org/10.1016/j.jcps.2014.08.002).

Denmark, F.L. (2010). Zeigarnik Effect. The Corsini Encyclopedia of Psychology (https://doi.org/10.1002/9780470479216.corpsy0924).

Heimbach, J.T. & Jacoby, J. (1972). The Zeigarnik Effect in Advertising. In: M. Venkatesan Ed.), SV-Proceedings of the Third Annual Conference of the Association for Consumer Research (pp.746-758). Chicago (IL): Association for Consumer Research.

Ryback, R. (2016, October 3). The Science of Accomplishing Your Goals. PsychologyToday (Accessed 9 July 2022, from https://www.psychologytoday.com/us/blog/the-truisms-wellness/201610/the-science-ac-complishing-your-goals).

Mehta, M. (2017, January 18). Why Our Brains Like Short-Term Goals. Entre-preneur (Accessed 4 July 2022, from https://www.entrepreneur.com/article/225356).

Chapter 3

Vaynerchuk, G. (2016). #AskGaryVee: One Entrepreneur's Take on Leader-ship, Social Media, and Self-Awareness. Harper Business.

Gary Vaynerchuk (2022, July 5). In Wikipedia (https://en.wikipedia.org/wiki/Gary_Vaynerchuk).

Elon Musk (2022, July 12). In Wikipedia (https://en.wikipedia.org/wiki/Elon_Musk).

Ruehle, R.C., Engelen, B. & Archer, A. (2021). Nudging Charitable Giving: What (If Anything) Is Wrong With It? Nonprofit and Voluntary Sector Quarterly, 50(2), 353-371 (https://doi.org/10.1177/0899764020954266).

Glocker, M.L., Langleben, D.D., Ruparel, K., Loughead, J.W., Gur, R.C., Sachser, N. (2009). Baby schema in infant faces induces cuteness per-ception and motivation for caretaking in adults. Ethology, 115(3), 257-263.

Froomle (s.d.). Bring smart personalisation to life with AI. Froomle.ai (Ac-cessed 12 July 2022, from https://www.froomle.ai/).

Drift (s.d.). Everything Starts With a Conversation. Drift.Com (Accessed July 12, 2022, from https://www.drift.com/).

MrBeast (2022, July 12). In Wikipedia (https://en.wikipedia.org/wiki/Mr-Beast).

YouTube star MrBeast breaks down how he makes eye-catching thumb-nails and why he'd pay $10,000 for the best possible one (2021, October 12). Business Insider (Accessed 12 July 2022, from https://www.busines-sinsider.com/mrbeast-youtube-thumbnail-strategy-advice-for-cre-ators-2021-10?international=true&r=US&IR=T).

Huapii (s.d.). Shape your future, empower your people. Huapii.Com (Ac-cessed July 12, 2022, from https://huapii.com/).

Qollabi (s.d.). Where joint action plans become predictable (Accessed 12 July 2022, from https://qollabi.com/).

Headlight (s.d.). Ambitious sales professionals for ambitious tech companies (Accessed July 12, 2022, from https://headlight.be/).

Tilroy (s.d.). Increase the value of your shop with omnichannel retail software (Accessed 12 July 2022, from https://www.tilroy.com/).

Wizata (s.d.). Industrial Manufacturing Software (Accessed July 12, 2022, from https://www.wizata.com/).

Humblet, M. (s.d.). Personal website. Michaelhumblet.com (Accessed 4 July 2022, from https://www.michaelhumblet.com).

Seaters (s.d.). A.I. Brand Relation Management. Seaters.Ai (Accessed 5 July 2022, from https://www.seaters.ai/).

Isaacson, W. (2015). Steve Jobs. Abacus.

Databroker (s.d.). The marketplace for data. Databroker.Global (Accessed 6 July 2022, from https://www.databroker.global/).

Social Seeder (s.d.). From employee engagement to employee advocacy. Socialseeder.Com (Accessed 12 July 2022, from https://www.social-seeder.com/en/).

Gartner (s.d.). Delivering Actionable, Objective Insight to Executives and Their Teams (Accessed July 12, 2022, from https://www.gartner.com/en).

Snauwaert, P. (2020, December 3). Whats on your mind (Podcast). Peter Snauwaert (Accessed 12 July 2022, from https://psgrow.podcastpage.io/).

Strobbo (s.d.). The flexible workforce planning tool! (Accessed 12 July 2022, from https://strobbo.com/).

Outsystems (s.d.). Low-code High-Performance Software Development. Outsystems.Com (Accessed 12 July 2022, from https://www.outsystems.com/).

Start it @KBC (s.d.). No-strings-attached-founder-centric startup accelerator by KBC. startit.be (Accessed 12 July 2022, from https://startit.be/).

Birdhouse (s.d.). Accelerator to Grow from start-up to scale-up. Birdhouse.Com (Accessed July 12, 2022, from https://gobirdhouse.com/en/).

Hubspot (s.d.). Inbound Marketing, Sales, and Service Software. Hubspot.Com (Accessed 12 July 2022, from https://www.hubspot.com/).

Microsoft (s.d.). Cloud, computing, apps, and games. Microsoft.com (Accessed 12 July 2022, from https://www.microsoft.com/nl-be/).

Bloovi (s.d.). Media company: Sometimes visionary, always directional. Bloovi.com (Accessed July 12, 2022, from https://www.bloovi.be/).

Barco (s.d.–b). The global technology leader that develops networked visualisation solutions for the entertainment, enterprise and healthcare markets. Barco.com (Accessed 12 July 2022, from https://www.barco.com/en/).

Radio 1 (2022, Feb 9). 'Eddy Wally was the founding father of behavioural economics' [Audio]. Radio 1 (https://radio1.be/luister/select/nieuwe-feiten/eddy-wally-was-de-founding-father-van-de-gedragseconomie#schuman).

NOS (2016, 24 March). Johan Cruijff, the language artist [Video]. YouTube (https://www.youtube.com/watch?v=HDqQAkdHDTk).

Dallos, D. (2011, April 20). Jurassic Park: heavy = expensive [Video]. YouTube (https://www.youtube.com/watch?v=OA1vmN-skXo).

ClickFunnelsTM (s.d.). Marketing Funnels Made Easy. ClickFunnels.Com (Accessed 12 July 2022, from https://www.clickfunnels.com/).

Foundr+ (s.d.). The global media and education company for entrepreneurs. Foundr.Com (Accessed July 12, 2022, from https://foundr.com/).

Sinek, S. (2011). Start with Why. Van Haren Publishing.

Parinello, A. (1999). Selling To Vito. Van Duuren Media.

Hitz, D. & Walsh, P. (2009, 1st ed.). How to Castrate a Bull: Unexpected Lessons on Risk, Growth, and Success in Business. Wiley.

Built to Sell: Creating a Business That Can Thrive Without You (2013). Penguin.

Chapter 4

Stampix (s.d.). Photo printing done in a flash. Stampix.Com (Accessed 12 July 2022, from https://stampix.com/en/).

http://www.michaelhumblet.com/whynow

Why Now [supporting material]. Michael Humblet (Accessed 12 July 2022, from https://michaelhumblet.com/whynow/).

Fisher, R., Ury, W. & Patton, B. (2012). Getting to Yes. Penguin Random House.

Dugdale, K. & Lambert, D. (2011, 2nd ed.). Smarter Selling: How to Build Sales by Building Trusted Relationships. Ft Pr.

Heath, C. & Heath, D. (2007, 1st ed.). Made to Stick: Why Some Ideas Survive and Others Die. Random House.

Trout, J. & Ries, A. (2001). Positioning: The Battle for Your Mind. McGraw-Hill Education.

Chapter 5

https://nobodyknowsyou.com/

Humblet, M. (2020, 1st ed.). Nobody knows you. Die Keure.

Brunson, R. (2020). Expert Secrets. Penguin Random House.

Holmes, C. & Levinson, J.C. (2008, 1st ed.). Ultimate Sales Machine. Penguin Putnam Inc.

Newport, C. (2012, 1st ed.). So Good They Can't Ignore You. Little, Brown & Company.

Vaynerchuk, G. (2013). Jab, Jab, Jab, Right Hook. HarperCollins.

Vaynerchuk, G. (2016). #AskGaryVee: One Entrepreneur's Take on Leadership, Social Media, and Self-Awareness. Harper Business.

Chapter 6

Qwilr (s.d.). Proposal Software and Templates - Quote Software. Qwilr.Com (Accessed 12 July 2022, from https://qwilr.com/).

Hough, K. (2014, 1st ed.). Be the Best Bad Presenter Ever: Break the Rules, Make Mistakes, and Win Them Over. Berrett-Koehler Publishers.

Hall, R. (2008). Brilliant Presentation. Prentice Hall.

Chapter 7

Why Now. [Supporting material]. Michael Humblet (Accessed 12 July 2022, from https://michaelhumblet.com/whynow/).

Humblet, M. [Michaelhumblet] (2017). Michael Humblet - YouTube channel [Video]. YouTube (https://www.youtube.com/michaelhumblet).

Humblet, M. (2021, June 21). #JustAskMichael - Ask all your Sales & Marketing questions [Video] YouTube (https://www.youtube.com/playlist?list=PLZN2P1oUXjCJQTENrV9GvOBLOQPMMw6Xe).

THE SALES STORY RULEBOOK

1. You control your prospect's **Attention** like a hypnotist controls his cobra. You make that attention peak at the beginning - with the right emotions - and again at the end.

2. The **Problem** gets a capital letter. You magnify it, make your prospect feel like you know it inside out. Focus on cause-and-effect, that is how you get your prospect to want to buy Now.

3. You gain **Trust** by putting social proof in your pitch. Subtly, throughout your Sales Story.

4. **Structure** gives your prospect peace of mind and speeds up your deal by undermining all their objections. 'Look how simple it is!'

Because you don't know if you're coming up with your proposal too early or on time, always give your prospect two **Next Actions:** a) Offer them a means to learn something about the problem they are struggling with. b) Let us solve your problem right away.

About the author

Michael Humblet has a thing for sales machines. He designs, builds, scales them and trains other salespeople to do the same. But before you are ready to do that, Humblet says you need to get your Sales Story right.

With his content agency Chaomatic.com, he has helped more than a thousand companies to scale up, his own included. He shares his knowledge, with pleasure, in his *Sales Acceleration* show on *YouTube* and in books. In his first book, *Nobody Knows You*, he shows how to build a content machine much like his own. Humblet's second book, *Why Now*, gives salespeople the tools they need to create their sales pitch; to get their Sales Story right.

Humblet is a board member at U-sights and the founder of The School of Sales. Before starting his own business, he spent 20 years knee-deep in business development and helped grow the revenues of software companies around the world. His business cards had titles like sales manager, sales director, VP of sales, head of global sales and even chief revenue officer. Humblet is a sought-after speaker at international conferences and a master storyteller, at least if you like stories with a twist. He loves writing, talking about gravity and going wild in his YouTube videos.

Connect with Michael Humblet on:

Website: https://michaelhumblet.com
Company: https://chaomatic.com
YouTube: https://www.youtube.com/michaelhumblet
LinkedIn: https://www.linkedin.com/in/michaelhumblet

JOIN THE
MOVEMENT

Post your picture with the cover now!

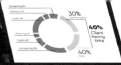

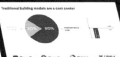
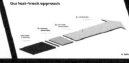

WHY NOW?

USE CODE

GOGOGO

**DOWNLOAD ALL EXAMPLES FROM THE BOOK AND
LEARN HOW TO APPLY *WHY NOW***

SCHOOLOFSALES.COM/WHYNOW/